Learning JAPANESE KANJI Practice Book

VOLUME 1

ERIKO SATO

TUTTLE Publishing

Tokyo | Rutland, Vermont | Singapore

“Books to Span the East and West”

Tuttle Publishing was founded in 1832 in the small New England town of Rutland, Vermont [USA]. Our core values remain as strong today as they were then—to publish best-in-class books which bring people together one page at a time. In 1948, we established a publishing outpost in Japan—and Tuttle is now a leader in publishing English-language books about the arts, languages and cultures of Asia. The world has become a much smaller place today and Asia's economic and cultural influence has grown. Yet the need for meaningful dialogue and information about this diverse region has never been greater. Over the past seven decades, Tuttle has published thousands of books on subjects ranging from martial arts and paper crafts to language learning and literature—and our talented authors, illustrators, designers and photographers have won many prestigious awards. We welcome you to explore the wealth of information available on Asia at **www.tuttlepublishing.com**.

Published by Tuttle Publishing, an imprint of Periplus Editions (HK) Ltd.

www.tuttlepublishing.com

ISBN: 978-0-8048-4493-2
ISBN: 978-4-8053-1377-0 (For sale in Japan only)

Distributed by:

North America, Latin America & Europe
Tuttle Publishing
364 Innovation Drive
North Clarendon, VT 05759-9436 U.S.A.
Tel: 1 (802) 773-8930
Fax: 1 (802) 773-6993
info@tuttlepublishing.com
www.tuttlepublishing.com

Japan
Tuttle Publishing
Yaekari Building, 3rd Floor
5-4-12 Osaki
Shinagawa-ku
Tokyo 141 0032
Tel: (81) 3 5437-0171; Fax: (81) 3 5437-0755
sales@tuttle.co.jp; www.tuttle.co.jp

Asia Pacific
Berkeley Books Pte. Ltd.
3 Kallang Sector #04-01
Singapore 349278
Tel: (65) 6741-2178; Fax: (65) 6741-2179
inquiries@periplus.com.sg; www.tuttlepublishing.com

First edition
30 29 28 27 26
16 15 14 13 12

Printed in China 2603CM

GPSR Representative, Matt Parsons matt.parsons@upi2mbooks.hr, UPI-2M PLUS d.o.o., Medulićeva 20, 10000 Zagreb, Croatia

Contents

Introduction

Modern Japanese can be written horizontally, from left to right, or vertically, from top to bottom. Japanese is one of the rare languages that uses multiple writing systems simultaneously, sometimes even in the same sentence. It is written by combining Chinese characters, called *kanji*, and two sets of syllabic alphabets called *kana* (*hiragana* and *katakana*) along with a few punctuation marks. Each kanji character represents a meaning, while each kana character represents a sound. For example, the following short sentence contains kanji, hiragana, and katakana:

パーティーに来ました。
Pātī ni kimashita.
(He) came to the party.

The non-Chinese loanword パーティー, written **pātī** in Roman letters and meaning *party*, is written in katakana. The stem of the verb 来, pronounced *ki* and meaning *to come*, is written using kanji. The grammatical particle に, written **ni** in Roman letters and meaning *to*, and the inflectional element ました, pronounced **mashita** (polite past affirmative), are written in hiragana. Isn't it interesting that all three writing systems can be used in such a simple sentence?

The total number of kana is relatively small: there are only 46 basic characters for each kana system in modern Japanese. By contrast, the total number of kanji is quite large. The Japanese government selected a total of 1,945 kanji (the so-called **jōyō** kanji, or kanji for daily use) in 1981. Japanese students are expected to learn how to read all of these kanji by the time they graduate high school. Additional kanji are used in proper names and certain other words.

You might think that there are too many kanji characters to learn, but don't get discouraged! If you learn the first several hundred kanji characters, you will be able to understand or guess the meaning of most street signs, restaurant menus, merchandise names, a variety of instructions, and much more! Furthermore, it is a lot of fun to learn kanji because the characters have interesting historical and cultural backgrounds and amazing compositional structures. Each kanji character has a unique meaning and shape, so each time you learn a new kanji character, you'll feel a bit like you've made a new friend.

The key to your ultimate success is to learn the basic kanji correctly and solidly. A thorough knowledge of the simplest kanji will provide you with a firm foundation for mastering more complex kanji quickly. The 103 kanji included in this book are the basic kanji used in everyday life and also commonly appear in Level 5 of the Japanese Language Proficiency Test. If you make a manageable plan for learning with this workbook everyday, you'll be able to enjoy the process of learning kanji and greatly improve your reading proficiency in Japanese. This introduction provides you with the basic information you need to know about the development and use of kanji and shows you how to write them properly.

How did kanji develop?

The word **kanji** literally means "characters of the Han Dynasty of ancient China" (206 B.C.E. to 220 A.D.) The initial forms of kanji originated in the Yellow River region of China between 2000 and 1500 B.C.E. The earliest preserved characters were written on tortoise shells and animal bones, and about 3,000 characters have been discovered from this early period. Depending on how they were formed, kanji can be classified into four main categories: pictorial kanji, indicative kanji, compound ideographic kanji, and phonetic-ideographic kanji.

Pictorial kanji originated from pictures of objects or phenomena. For example:

Meaning	Original Picture	Modern Kanji
River		川
Mountain		山
Tree		木
Sun		日
Moon		月
Rain		雨

Indicative kanji were created as symbolic representations of abstract concepts using points and lines. For example:

Meaning	Original Sign	Modern Kanji
One		一
Two		二
Three		三
Top		上
Bottom		下

Compound ideographic kanji were formed by combining two or more pictorial or indicative kanji to bring out a new but simple idea. For example:

Meaning	Combining Multiple Kanji	Resulting Kanji
Woods	木 + 木 tree + tree	林
Forest	木 + 木 + 木 tree + tree + tree	森
Bright	日 + 月 sun + moon	明

Finally, *phonetic-ideographic kanji* were formed by combining an element that expressed meaning and an element that carried the sound. For example, the following characters all stand for some body of water:

Meaning	Combining Elements	Kanji
Inlet	氵 + 工 *water* + KŌ	江
Ocean	氵 + 羊 *water* + YŌ	洋
River	氵 + 可 *water* + KA	河

The left side of each character above, 氵, contributes the meaning, showing that each kanji's meaning is related to water. The right side of each character 工, 羊, or 可, contributes the sound, showing how the kanji should be pronounced.

Kanji characters were brought to Japan from China between the fourth and the fifth centuries A.D. Until then, there were no written symbols in Japanese. The Japanese initially developed a hybrid system where kanji were given Japanese pronunciations and were used for writing Japanese. This system proved unwieldy, since Japanese and Chinese grammar and structure are so different. Then, they developed a system, **man'yōgana**, in which a limited set of kanji was used to write Japanese words with their sounds. Hiragana and katakana were developed in the Heian Period (794-1185) from some of the kanji characters included in **man'yōgana**. About 2,000 kanji as well as hiragana and katakana are still used in modern Japanese. Interestingly, there are some kanji characters that were created in Japan. For example, the kanji 峠 (mountain pass), 畑 (field of crops), and 働 (work) were all created in Japan by combining multiple existing kanji components.

How are kanji pronounced?

The Japanese language is very different from the Chinese language, having very distinct grammar and sounds. Many Chinese words consist of one syllable, but most Japanese words have more than one syllable. So, the assignment of a Japanese pronunciation to each kanji required both flexibility and creativity.

On-readings and kun-readings

There are two different ways of reading kanji in Japanese: on-readings (or **on-yomi**) and kun-readings (or **kun-yomi**). When kanji characters were first introduced to Japan, the original Chinese pronunciations were also adapted with only minor modifications. Such Chinese ways of reading kanji are called on-readings and are still used, especially when a character appears as a part of a compound where two or more kanji are combined to form a word.

At the same time, many kanji characters were assigned the pronunciation of the existing native Japanese word whose meaning was closest to that of the character. Such Japanese readings are called kun-readings, and are used especially when a character occurs independently in a sentence. For example, the character 母 is pronounced **bo** (on-reading) when used as a part of the compound word 母国, **bokoku** (mother country), but is pronounced **haha** (kun-reading) when used by itself. This is illustrated in the following sentence.

私の母の母国はフランスです。
Watashi no haha no bokoku wa Furansu desu.
My mother's mother country is France.

In this workbook, on-readings are shown in katakana and, when Romanized, in upper-case letters. Conversely, kun-readings are shown in hiragana and in lower-case letters when Romanized.

Some kanji characters have more than one on-reading or kun-reading, and different readings are used in different contexts. Also note that there are special cases where it is not possible to clearly divide a kanji compound into components that can be pronounced separately.

Okurigana

As noted above, many Chinese words consist of a single syllable, expressed by only one Chinese character, but the corresponding Japanese words often have more than one syllable. In order to use kanji in the Japanese language, some kanji characters needed to be accompanied by kana. Such kana are called **okurigana**. Okurigana are particularly important for verbs and adjectives, which need inflectional elements, although they may also be used for other types of words, including nouns and adverbs. For example, in the following words, the kanji 高, meaning *expensive* or *high*, and the kana that follow jointly represent the pronunciation of the whole word, successfully representing its complete meaning:

高い	**takai**	expensive (plain present affirmative)
高くない	**takakunai**	not expensive (plain present negative)
高かった	**takakatta**	was expensive (plain past affirmative)

In this book, the okurigana are preceded by "–" when first presented in kun-readings.

Furigana

Kanji characters are occasionally provided with kana that shows how they are intended to be read in the given context. Such kana used as a pronunciation guide are called **furigana**. For example, the hiragana characters placed right above the kanji in the following word are furigana:

たか
高い

Furigana is often used for children or learners of Japanese. This can be a great help for you at the beginning! It is also used in newspapers for unusual readings and for characters not included in the officially recognized set of essential kanji. Japanese comic books use furigana generously!

How are kanji used in compounds?

Some Japanese words are represented by only one kanji (e.g., 赤, **aka**, *red*), but many Japanese words are represented by a kanji with okurigana (e.g., 高い, **takai** *expensive*) or by a kanji compound. Kanji compounds constitute a large proportion of Japanese vocabulary. For example, 先生, written **sensei** in Roman letters, is a compound meaning *teacher*. It consists of two characters, 先 (ahead) and 生 (live). In general, on-readings are used for compounds, but occasionally, kun-readings are also used.

By the way, when you write a compound, there is no need to add a space between the kanji characters in it, but don't try to squeeze the characters together to fit in one-character space. Each character in a compound should take one-character space. For example, notice the difference between 女子(girl) and 好(to like). The first item (女子) is a kanji compound that consists of two kanji characters, 女(woman) and 子(child). By contrast, the second item (好) is a single kanji character that consists of two kanji components, 女and 子.

Some kanji compounds were created in Japan and have been brought back to China and are now being used there. Examples include 電話 **denwa** (telephone), 化学 **kagaku** (science), and 社会 **shakai** (society). Many kanji compounds are also used to represent Japanese culture, concepts, and ideas (e.g., 神道 **Shinto**) as well as to name Japanese people (e.g., 田中 **Tanaka**), institutions and companies (e.g., 三菱 **Mitsubishi**), places (e.g., 東京 **Tokyo**), and eras (e.g., 明治 **Meiji**). Regardless of their origin, kanji compounds form an essential part of the lives of Japanese people.

There are two special cases where you may have a hard time reading kanji compounds: **jukujikun** and **ateji**. A **jukujikun** is a unique kun-reading assigned to an entire kanji compound rather than to each kanji character separately. For example, the compound 明日 (tomorrow) can be read as **myōnichi** using the on-reading of each character in the compound one after another, as in the majority of typical kanji compounds, but can also be read as **asu**, which is a **jukujikun**. In the latter case, it is impossible to tell which syllable corresponds to 明 and which syllable corresponds to 日 because the reading is assigned to the whole compound. Other examples of **jukujikun** include 一日 **tsuitachi** (the first day of the month), 五月雨 **samidare** (early summer rain), 海老 **ebi** (shrimp), and 土産 **miyage** (souvenir).

Ateji are kanji characters whose sounds are used to represent native Japanese words or non-Chinese loanwords regardless of the meanings of the kanji. For example, the kanji compound 寿司 is made of **ateji**. It is pronounced **sushi**, and means sushi, the food, even though 寿 means *one's natural life span* and 司 means *to administer*, neither of which are directly related to food. Other examples of **ateji** include 目出度い **medetai** (happy), 出鱈目 **detarame** (random), and 珈琲 **kōhī** (coffee). Many **ateji** for non-Chinese loanwords, including proper names, have been replaced by katakana, but some are still used. In addition, new **ateji** are occasionally created.

What are radicals?

Most kanji characters are composed of two or more components. Each component may contribute to the kanji's meaning, sound, or merely its shape. For example, 日 is an independent kanji character meaning *sun*, but is also a component that lends meaning to many kanji. For example:

明 *bright*　　時 *time*　　晴 *clear up*

There are many kanji-components, but the most basic and identifiable elements of kanji are called *radicals*. For hundreds of years, Chinese dictionaries have organized kanji characters according to their radicals. Each Chinese character was assigned a radical and placed in an appropriate section of a dictionary according to the designated radical.

It is not always clear which component of a kanji is the radical, but this workbook shows the radical for each kanji at the upper right corner of the page. Whenever you learn a new kanji using this book, check its radical. It will help you understand and remember the meaning and the internal composition of the kanji. Eventually, you will be able to identify the radical just by looking at a kanji. There is an index of characters organized by radical near the end of this book.

Depending on its position in a kanji character, radicals are classified into seven categories, as shown in the chart on page 8.

How do I look up a kanji in a Japanese dictionary?

Many dictionaries list kanji characters according to their pronunciation, for both on-readings and kun-readings, either in kana or in Roman letters. So, if you know the reading of a kanji character, you can easily find it in such a dictionary using its pronunciation-based index. For example, *The Original Modern Reader's Japanese-English Character Dictionary* by Andrew N. Nelson (Tuttle Publishing), has an on/kun index in the back, and kanji characters are alphabetically listed according to both their on-readings and their kun-readings in Roman letters with a unique code number provided for each character. Using that code number, you can easily find the page you should go to in the dictionary.

What if you see a kanji, but you don't know how to read it? You could then use the radical index included in most dictionaries. In a radical index, hundreds of radicals are listed according to the radical's total number of strokes. For example, 日 is the radical of 明, and it has 4 strokes. You can find the radical 日 in the radical list under the section for four-stroke radicals in just a few seconds. There you will find a code number, which will guide you to the list of all the kanji with the radical 日. For example, you will see many kanji, including 明, 晴, and 時, on the page specified by the code number for the radical 日. They are ordered according to their total stroke count. You can easily find the kanji character you want in the list.

If you have no clue about either the pronunciation or the radical of the kanji, you can use the kanji's total stroke count as a reference. This book specifies the total stroke count for each kanji at the upper left corner of the box containing the kanji, but if you always write kanji in the correct stroke order and with the correct stroke count, you can figure it out by yourself.

How are kanji characters written?

To write kanji properly and legibly, it is very important to know how each stroke in a kanji is drawn. Here are some principles and tendencies for stroke endings, stroke directions, and stroke orders.

Stroke Endings

Each stroke ends in とめ **tome** (stop), はね **hane** (jump), or はらい **harai** (sweep). (Note that some diagonal lines end in stop-sweep.) For example, a vertical straight line can end in stop, jump, or sweep, as shown below:

とめ **tome** (stop)　　はね **hane** (jump)　　はらい **harai** (sweep)

Stroke Directions

A stroke can be vertical, horizontal, diagonal, angled, or curved, or can be just a short abbreviated line.

Vertical lines always go from top to bottom, and *horizontal lines* always go from left to right.

Name	Position		Example	
偏 **hen** (lit., partial, one-sided)	left		亻	にんべん **ninben** (person) 休 (rest), 体(body), 作(make)
旁 **tsukuri** (lit., aside)	right		斤	おのづくり **onozukuri** (ax) 近 (near), 新 (new), 所 (place)
冠 **kanmuri** (lit., crown)	top		艹	くさかんむり **kusakanmuri** (grass) 草 (grass), 花 (flower), 茶 (tea)
脚 **ashi** (lit., leg)	bottom		儿	ひとあし **hitoashi** (human legs) 見 (look), 兄 (older brother), 先 (ahead)
構 **kamae** (lit., enclosure)	frame		口	くにがまえ **kunigamae** (border) 国 (country), 困 (be in difficulty), 囚 (prisoner)
			門	もんがまえ **mongamae** (gate) 問 (inquire), 聞 (listen), 間 (between)
			凵	うけばこ **ukebako** (container, vessel) 画 (picture), 凶 (bad), 歯 (tooth)
			匚	かくしがまえ **kakushigamae** (conceal) 区 (ward), 医 (physician), 匿 (conceal)
			勹	つつみがまえ **tsutsumigamae** (wrap) 包 (wrap), 抱 (embrace), 句 (phrase)
垂 **tare** (lit., something hanging down)	top & left		疒	やまいだれ **yamaidare** (sickness) 病 (illness), 痛 (painful), 癌 (cancer)
繞 **nyō, nyū** (lit., going around)	left & bottom		辶	しんにょう **shinnyō** (proceed) 道 (road), 進 (proceed), 過 (pass)

Diagonal lines can go either downward or upward. For example:

If a stroke forms a corner, a sharp angle, or a curve, it goes from left to right and then goes down, or goes down and then left to right. For example:

corner

sharp angle

curve

Some strokes have a combination of a sharp angle and a curve. For example:

Some strokes are extremely short and are called てん **ten**. They may be vertical or slightly diagonal:

Stroke Order

You should remember how the strokes in each character are ordered in order to write a character neatly with the appropriate shape. Most kanji characters are written following the general principles of stroke order:

1. Kanji are written from top to bottom.

三 (three) 

2. Kanji are written from left to right.

川 (river) 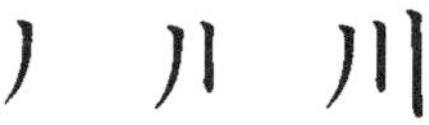

3. Horizontal strokes usually precede vertical strokes when crossing, although there are some exceptions such as 王 and 田.

十 (ten) 

4. A central line usually precedes the strokes placed on its right and left.

小 (small) 

5. An outer frame must be written first before finishing the inside except for the bottom line. The bottom line of an outer frame must be completed at the very end.

国 (country) 

6. A right-to-left diagonal stroke precedes a left-to-right diagonal stroke.

人 (person) 

7. A vertical line piercing through the center of a character is written last.

車 (vehicle) 

8. A horizontal line piercing the center of the character is written last.

子 (child) 

How do I learn to write kanji?

Remember that a good beginning and good planning are the keys to success in learning kanji. The following are some suggested steps for learning kanji using this workbook.

Get used to the strokes

Before writing any kanji, practice drawing some of the simple strokes with different endings many times on a sheet of scrap paper. For example, try drawing the strokes presented above (e.g., vertical lines, diagonal lines). Each time you end the stroke, say とめ **tome** (stop), はね **hane** (jump), or はらい **harai** (sweep), depending on which type of ending you are working on. If you have a brush and ink, try to make changes in the thickness of different portions of each stroke. Of course, you can also use a pen or pencil. If you do, ignore the difference in the thickness of different portions of each stroke. Just get used to the general flow of strokes. It will help you to write kanji beautifully in an authentic style.

Understand the character

Before writing an actual kanji character as a whole, familiarize yourself with its meaning, pronunciation, usage examples, and radical. Be creative and make associations to help you remember the shape, composition, meaning, and sound of the character you are working on. Your associations can be logical or natural, or can be silly or funny. Your imagination and creativity will always help you learn and remember new things, especially when you are dealing with numerous items. Under each character in this book, the first several boxes show the stroke order and direction. Refer to them, and try writing the character once. The number of strokes for each kanji is specified in the upper-left corner of each page. Check whether you used the correct number of strokes when you wrote the kanji. Then compare your character with the one printed on the page. Pay attention to the size and the position of the character in relation with the box as well as the proportion and shape of the lines.

Practice writing the character

When you have fully understood the given character in terms of meaning, pronunciation, usage, radical, and stroke order, write it about 10 times in a row. You may not believe it, but your hand muscle will remember how to write a kanji if you repeat writing it many times. If helpful, trace over the gray characters at the beginning of each page.

Review kanji periodically

Practice a few new characters at a time every day following the above steps. Once you have worked your way through the first half of the book, in which the kanji are introduced for the first time, move on to the practice exercises in the second half of the book. These practice exercises will allow you to use the 103 kanji you have learned, plus your existing knowledge of hiragana and katakana, to write real vocabulary words, which is a great way to reinforce and remember the kanji. Each exercise gives particular emphasis to the four kanji given in the heading, and you should find that as you work your way through the exercises that your writing becomes smoother and your recall of the characters easier. The more vocabulary words you learn, and the more you practice writing them, the easier it becomes to memorize the kanji!

頑張ってください。
Ganbatte kudasai!
Try your best (and good luck)!

一

(1 stroke)

meaning
one

radical
一

ON readings
イチ **ICHI**, イッ **I'**

KUN readings
ひと– **hito-**,
ひと–つ **hito-tsu**

common words

一人	ひとり	**hitori**	one person
一日	いちにち/ ついたち	**ichinichi/ tsuitachi**	a day; all day/ the first day (of the month)
一つ	ひとつ	**hitotsu**	one (piece; age)
一月	いちがつ	**ichigatsu**	January

二

(2 strokes)

meaning
two

radical
二

ON readings
ニ **NI**

KUN readings
ふた **futa**,
ふた–つ **futa-tsu**

common words

二月	にがつ	**nigatsu**	February
二人	ふたり	**futari**	two people
二日	ふつか	**futsuka**	two days, 2nd day of the month
二千	にせん	**nisen**	two thousand
二つ	ふたつ	**futatsu**	two (pieces; age)

三

(3 strokes)

meaning
three

radical
一

ON readings
サン **SAN**

KUN readings
み **mi-**,
み(っ)–つ **mi(t)-tsu**

common words

三月	さんがつ	**sangatsu**	March
三日	みっか	**mikka**	three days, 3rd day of the month
三人	さんにん	**san'nin**	three people
三つ	みっつ	**mittsu**	three (pieces; age)

四

(5 strokes)

meaning
four

radical
囗

ON readings
シ **SHI**

KUN readings
よ **yo,** よ(っ)-つ **yo(t)-tsu,** よん **yon**

common words

四月	しがつ	**shigatsu**	April
四日	よっか	**yokka**	four days, 4th of the month
四人	よにん	**yonin**	four people
四回	よんかい	**yonkai**	four times
四千	よんせん	**yonsen**	four thousand
四つ	よっつ	**yottsu**	four (pieces; age)

五

(4 strokes)

meaning
five

radical
二

ON readings
ゴ **GO**

KUN readings
いつ **itsu,** いつ-つ **itsu-tsu**

common words

五日	いつか	**itsuka**	five days, 5th day of the month
五月	ごがつ	**gogatsu**	May
五千	ごせん	**gosen**	five thousand
五十	ごじゅう	**gojū**	fifty
五百	ごひゃく	**gohyaku**	five hundred
五つ	いつつ	**itsutsu**	five (pieces; age)

六

(4 strokes)

meaning
six

radical
八

ON readings
ロク **ROKU**

KUN readings
む **mu**, む(っ)-つ **mu(t)-tsu**

common words

六日　むいか **muika** six days, 6th day of the month
六月　ろくがつ **rokugatsu** June
六年生　ろくねんせい **rokunensei** sixth grader
六時　ろくじ **rokuji** six o'clock
六百　ろっぴゃく **roppyaku** six hundred
六十　ろくじゅう **rokujū** sixty
六つ　むっつ **muttsu** six (pieces; age)

六 六 六

七

(2 strokes)

meaning
seven

radical
一

ON readings
シチ **SHICHI**

KUN readings
なな **nana**, なな-つ **nana-tsu**

common words

七月　しちがつ **shichigatsu** July
七人　なな/しちにん **nana/shichinin** seven people
七日　なのか **nanoka** seven days, 7th of the month
七万円　ななまんえん **nanaman'en** seventy thousand yen
七時　しちじ **shichiji** seven o'clock
七百　ななひゃく **nanahyaku** seven hundred
七つ　ななつ **nanatsu** seven (pieces; age)

七 七 七

八

(2 strokes)

meaning
eight

radical
八

ON readings
ハチ **HACHI**

KUN readings
や **ya**, や(っ)-つ **ya(t)-tsu**

common words

八月	はちがつ	**hachigatsu**	August
八日	ようか	**yōka**	eight days, 8th of the month
八時	はちじ	**hachiji**	eight o'clock
八十	はちじゅう	**hachijū**	eighty
八百	はっぴゃく	**happyaku**	eight hundred
八つ	やっつ	**yattsu**	eight (pieces; age)
八百屋	やおや	**yaoya**	greengrocer's

ノ 1 八 2 八 八 八

九

(2 strokes)

meaning
nine

radical
乙 (乚)

ON readings
ク **KU**, キュウ **KYŪ**

KUN readings
ここの-つ **kokono-tsu**, ここの **kokono**

common words

九月	くがつ	**kugatsu**	September
九人	きゅうにん	**kyūnin**	nine people
九日	ここのか	**kokonoka**	nine days, 9th of the month
九時	くじ	**kuji**	nine o'clock
九十	きゅうじゅう	**kyūjū**	ninety
九百	きゅうひゃく	**kyūhyaku**	nine hundred
九つ	ここのつ	**kokonotsu**	nine (pieces; age)

ノ 1 九 2 九 九 九

十

(2 strokes)

meaning
ten

radical
十

ON readings
ジュウ **JŪ**, ジッ **JI'**

KUN readings
とお **tō**

common words
十一　じゅういち **jūichi** eleven
十月　じゅうがつ **jūgatsu** October
十日　とおか **tōka** ten days; 10th of the month
二十歳　はたち **hatachi** twenty years old
二十日　はつか **hatsuka** twenty days; 20th of the month
十一月　じゅういちがつ **jūichigatsu** November
十二月　じゅうにがつ **jūnigatsu** December

一 十 十 十 十

百

(6 strokes)

meaning
hundred

radical
白

ON readings
ヒャク **HYAKU**

KUN readings

common words
三百　さんびゃく **sanbyaku** three hundred
百円　ひゃくえん **hyakuen** one hundred yen
百人　ひゃくにん **hyakunin** one hundred people
何百　なんびゃく **nanbyaku** how many hundreds
百本　ひゃっぽん **hyappon** one hundred (trees, bottles, or long thin things)
百枚　ひゃくまい **hyakumai** one hundred sheets (of …)

一 丆 丅 百 百 百 百 百 百

千	meaning	ON readings	common words
(3 strokes)	thousand radical 十	セン **SEN** KUN readings ち **chi**	三千　さんぜん　**sanzen**　three thousand 千円　せんえん　**sen'en**　one thousand yen 千人　せんにん　**sen'nin**　one thousand people 五千円　ごせんえん　**gosen'en**　five thousand yen 二千年　にせんねん　**nisen'nen**　two thousand years 千代紙　ちよがみ　**chiyogami**　origami paper with colored figures

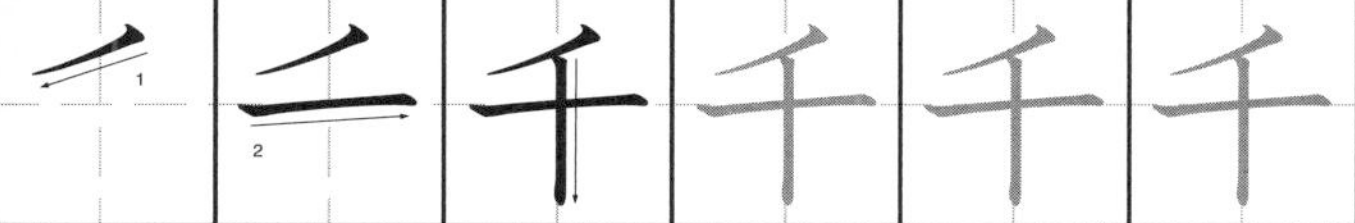

万	meaning	ON readings	common words
(3 strokes)	ten thousand radical 一	マン **MAN**, バン **BAN** KUN readings	一万円　いちまんえん　**ichiman'en**　ten thousand yen 一万人　いちまんにん　**ichiman'nin**　ten thousand people 十万　じゅうまん　**jūman**　one hundred thousand 億万長者　おくまんちょうじゃ　**okumanchōja**　billionaire 百万円　ひゃくまんえん　**hyakuman'en**　one million yen

円

(4 strokes)

meaning
circle; yen (Japanese monetary unit)

radical
冂

ON readings
エン **EN**

KUN readings
まる-い **maru-i**

common words

円高	えんだか	**endaka**	high value of the yen
円安	えんやす	**en'yasu**	low value of the yen
円周	えんしゅう	**enshū**	circumference
半円	はんえん	**han'en**	semicircle
楕円	だえん	**da'en**	oval
十円	じゅうえん	**jūen**	ten yen
円満な	えんまんな	**enman na**	harmonious

曜

(18 strokes)

meaning
days of the week

radical
日

ON readings
ヨウ **YŌ**

KUN readings

common words

何曜日	なんようび	**nan'yōbi**	what day of the week
月曜日	げつようび	**getsuyōbi**	Monday
火曜日	かようび	**kayōbi**	Tuesday
水曜日	すいようび	**suiyōbi**	Wednesday
木曜日	もくようび	**mokuyōbi**	Thursday
金曜日	きんようび	**kin'yōbi**	Friday
土曜日	どようび	**doyōbi**	Saturday

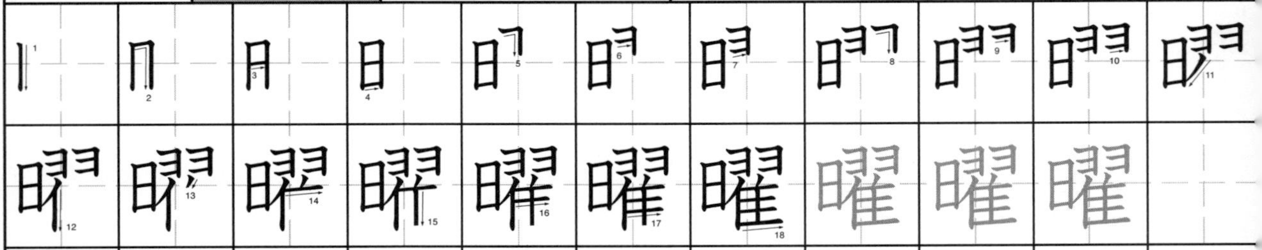

週 (11 strokes)	meaning week radical ⻌	ON readings シュウ **SHŪ** KUN readings	common words 今週　こんしゅう　**konshū**　this week 週日　しゅうじつ　**shūjitsu**　weekday 先週　せんしゅう　**senshū**　last week 来週　らいしゅう　**raishū**　next week 毎週　まいしゅう　**maishū**　every week 三週間　さんしゅうかん　**sanshūkan**　(a period of) three weeks

年 (6 strokes)	meaning year; age radical 干	ON readings ネン **NEN** KUN readings とし **toshi**	common words 毎年　まいねん/まいとし　**mainen/maitoshi**　every year 一年間　いちねんかん　**ichinenkan**　(a period of) one year 今年　ことし　**kotoshi**　this year 来年　らいねん　**rainen**　next year 年中　ねんじゅう　**nenjū**　throughout the year 年下　としした　**toshishita**　younger 年上　としうえ　**toshiue**　older, senior

日

(4 strokes)

meaning	ON readings	common words
sun; day; counter for days	ニチ **NICHI**, ジツ **JITSU**	誕生日　たんじょうび　**tanjōbi**　birthday
radical 日	**KUN readings** ひ **hi**, か **ka**	毎日　まいにち　**mainichi**　every day
		日本　にほん/にっぽん　**nihon/nippon**　Japan
		明日　あす　**asu**　tomorrow
		日の出前　ひのでまえ　**hinode mae**　before sunrise

月

(4 strokes)

meaning	ON readings	common words
month; moon	ガツ **GATSU**, ゲツ **GETSU**	今月　こんげつ　**kongetsu**　this month
radical 月	**KUN readings** つき **tsuki**	生年月日　せいねんがっぴ　**seinengappi**　date of birth
		先月　せんげつ　**sengetsu**　last month
		来月　らいげつ　**raigetsu**　next month
		毎月　まいげつ/まいつき　**maigetsu/matsuki**　every month

火	meaning	ON readings	common words
(4 strokes)	fire **radical** 火	カ **KA** **KUN readings** ひ **hi**, ほ **ho**	火山　かざん　**kazan**　volcano 火事　かじ　**kaji**　fire 花火　はなび　**hanabi**　fireworks 火花　ひばな　**hibana**　spark 噴火　ふんか　**funka**　volcanic eruption 火星　かせい　**kasei**　Mars

水	meaning	ON readings	common words
(4 strokes)	water **radical** 水	スイ **SUI** **KUN readings** みず **mizu**	香水　こうすい　**kōsui**　perfume お水　おみず　**o-mizu**　water 噴水　ふんすい　**funsui**　fountain 水分　すいぶん　**suibun**　moisture 水泳　すいえい　**suiei**　swimming

木 (4 strokes)	**meaning** tree, wood **radical** 木	**ON readings** モク **MOKU,** ボク **BOKU** **KUN readings** き **ki,** こ **ko**	**common words** 木かげ　こかげ　**kokage**　the shade of the tree 大木　たいぼく　**taiboku**　big tree 木造　もくぞう　**mokuzō**　wooden, made of wood 高い木　たかいき　**takai ki**　tall tree 木の下　きのした　**ki no shita**　under a tree 木星　もくせい　**mokusei**　Jupiter

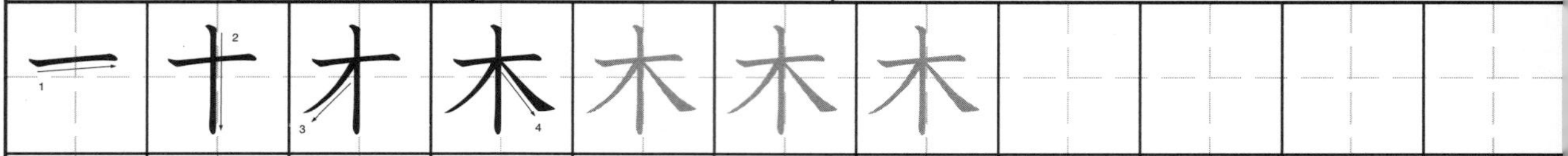

金 (8 strokes)	**meaning** gold, metal; money **radical** 金	**ON readings** キン **KIN,** コン **KON** **KUN readings** かな **kana,** かね **kane**	**common words** お金　おかね　**okane**　money 針金　はりがね　**harigane**　wire 金メダル　きんメダル　**kinmedaru**　gold medal 前金　まえきん　**maekin**　advance (money) 金属　きんぞく　**kinzoku**　metal

土

(3 strokes)

meaning	ON readings	common words
earth, soil	ド **DO**, ト **TO**	土木工事　どぼくこうじ　**dobokukōji**　public works
	KUN readings	土地　とち　**tochi**　ground, plot of land
	つち **tsuchi**	土間　どま　**doma**　dirt floor (in traditional house)
radical		土手　どて　**dote**　embankment
土		土足で　どそくで　**dosoku de**　with footwear on
		土と水　つちとみず　**tsuchi to mizu**　soil and water

午

(4 strokes)

meaning	ON readings	common words
noon	ゴ **GO**	午後　ごご　**gogo**　afternoon, P.M.
	KUN readings	午前　ごぜん　**gozen**　morning, A.M.
		午前中　ごぜんちゅう　**gozenchū**　all morning
radical		正午　しょうご　**shōgo**　noon
十		午後二時　ごごにじ　**gogo niji**　two o’clock, two P. M.

今

(4 strokes)

meaning
now, the present

radical
人

ON readings
コン **KON,** キン **KIN**

KUN readings
いま **ima**

common words

今すぐ	いますぐ	**imasugu**	right now
今日	きょう	**kyō**	today
今朝	けさ	**kesa**	this morning
今回	こんかい	**konkai**	this time
今度	こんど	**kondo**	next time
今晩	こんばん	**konban**	tonight

分

(4 strokes)

meaning
to divide; portion; minute

radical
刀

ON readings
ブン **BUN,** フン **FUN**

KUN readings
わ-ける **wa-keru,**
わ-かる **wa-karu**

common words

三日分	みっかぶん	**mikkabun**	three days' worth
四分	よんぷん	**yonpun**	four minutes
自分	じぶん	**jibun**	self
多分	たぶん	**tabun**	perhaps
分かる	わかる	**wakaru**	to understand
分ける	わける	**wakeru**	to divide

半	meaning	ON readings	common words
(5 strokes)	half **radical** 十	ハン **HAN** **KUN readings** なか-ば **naka-ba**	一時半 いちじはん **ichijihan** half past one 半年 はんとし **hantoshi** six months 半日 はんにち **han'nichi** half a day 半分 はんぶん **hanbun** half 半月 はんつき **hantsuki** half a month 半ば なかば **nakaba** middle, halfway

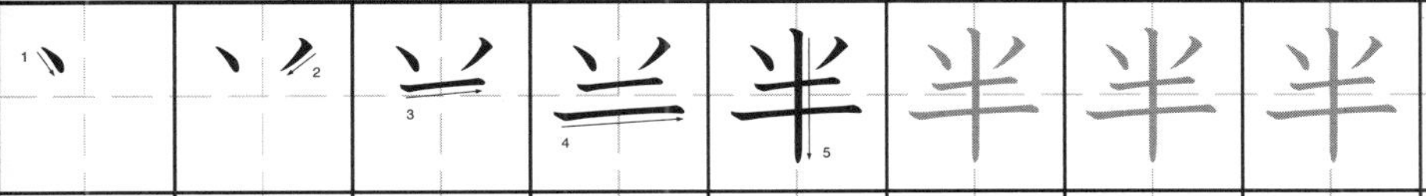

毎	meaning	ON readings	common words
(6 strokes)	every, each **radical** 毋	マイ **MAI** **KUN readings** ごと **goto**	毎朝 まいあさ **maiasa** every morning 毎晩 まいばん **maiban** every night 日毎に ひごとに **higoto ni** daily 毎に ごとに **goto ni** one by one, every 年毎に としごとに **toshigoto ni** annually 半年毎に はんとしごとに **hantoshigoto ni** bi-annually 毎時 まいじ **maiji** every hour

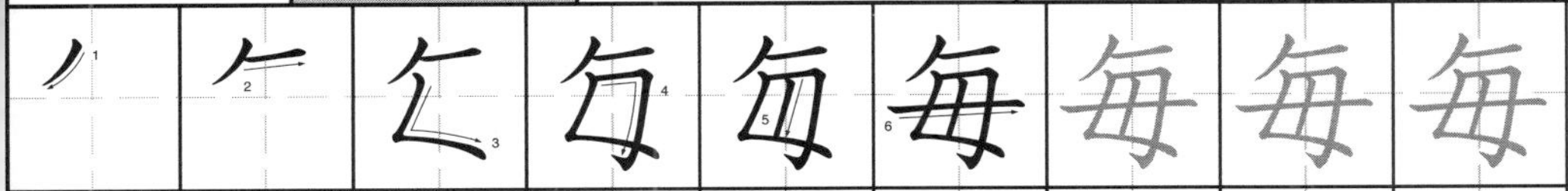

何

(7 strokes)

meaning
what, how many

radical
亻

ON readings
カ **KA**

KUN readings
なに **nani**, なん **nan**

common words

何回	なんかい	**nankai**	how many times
何月	なんがつ	**nangatsu**	what month
何年	なんねん	**nan'nen**	what year; how many years
何時	なんじ	**nanji**	what time
何人	なんにん	**nan'nin**	how many people
何分	なんぷん	**nanpun**	how many minutes

時

(10 strokes)

meaning
hour; time

radical
日

ON readings
ジ **JI**

KUN readings
とき **toki**

common words

一時間	いちじかん	**ichijikan**	one hour
時間	じかん	**jikan**	time, hour
時代	じだい	**jidai**	period (of time), era, age
当時	とうじ	**tōji**	at that time
同時に	どうじに	**dōji ni**	at the same time
日時	にちじ	**nichiji**	the date and time
時間外	じかんがい	**jikangai**	overtime

計

(9 strokes)

meaning
to measure; to plan, to arrange

radical
言

ON readings
ケイ **KEI**

KUN readings
はか-る **haka-ru**, はか-らう **haka-rau**

common words
計画する　けいかくする　**keikaku suru**　to plan
時計　とけい　**tokei**　watch, clock
温度計　おんどけい　**ondokei**　thermometer
合計する　ごうけいする　**gōkei suru**　to total, to add up
小計　しょうけい　**shōkei**　subtotal
計る　はかる　**hakaru**　to measure

計 計 計

間

(12 strokes)

meaning
between; space, interval

radical
門

ON readings
カン **KAN**, ケン **KEN**

KUN readings
あいだ **aida**, ま **ma**

common words
仲間　なかま　**nakama**　partner, friend
年間の　ねんかんの　**nenkan no**　annual
何週間　なんしゅうかん　**nanshūkan**　how many weeks
何日間　なんにちかん　**nan'nichikan**　how many days
居間　いま　**ima**　living room
この間　このあいだ　**kono aida**　the other day
人間　にんげん　**ningen**　human being

間 間 間 間 間

男

(7 strokes)

meaning
man, male

radical
田

ON readings
ダン **DAN**, ナン **NAN**

KUN readings
おとこ **otoko**

common words
男の子　おとこのこ　**otoko no ko**　boy
次男　じなん　**jinan**　second son
男子　だんし　**danshi**　man, boy
男らしい　おとこらしい　**otoko rashii**　masculine
男女　だんじょ　**danjo**　men and women
男性　だんせい　**dansei**　man
長男　ちょうなん　**chōnan**　eldest son

女

(3 strokes)

meaning
woman, female

radical
女

ON readings
ジョ **JO**, ニョ **NYO**, ニョウ **NYŌ**

KUN readings
おんな **on'na**, め **me**

common words
少女　しょうじょ　**shōjo**　girl
女王　じょおう　**jo'ō**　queen
女性　じょせい　**josei**　woman
女子　じょし　**joshi**　woman, girl
女子大　じょしだい　**joshidai**　women's university
女の子　おんなのこ　**on'na no ko**　girl
女神　めがみ　**megami**　goddess

父

(4 strokes)

meaning
father

radical
父

ON readings
フ **FU**

KUN readings
ちち **chichi**

common words

お父さん　おとうさん　**otōsan**　father
父親　ちちおや　**chichioya**　father
父母　ふぼ　**fubo**　father and mother, parents
義父　ぎふ　**gifu**　father-in-law
父上　ちちうえ　**chichiue**　father (archaic)
父子　ふし　**fushi**　father and child
父の日　ちちのひ　**chichi no hi**　Father's Day

母

(5 strokes)

meaning
mother

radical
母

ON readings
ボ **BO**

KUN readings
はは **haha**

common words

お母さん　おかあさん　**okāsan**　mother
母親　ははおや　**hahaoya**　mother
母国　ぼこく　**bokoku**　mother country
母国語　ぼこくご　**bokokugo**　mother tongue
母上　ははうえ　**hahaue**　mother (archaic)
母の日　ははのひ　**haha no hi**　Mother's Day

子

(3 strokes)

meaning
child

radical
子

ON readings
シ **SHI,** ス **SU**

KUN readings
こ **ko**

common words

帽子　ぼうし　**bōshi**　hat
息子　むすこ　**musuko**　son
椅子　いす　**isu**　chair
子ども　こども　**kodomo**　child
子会社　こがいしゃ　**kogaisha**　subsidiary company

友

(4 strokes)

meaning
friend

radical
又

ON readings
ユウ **YŪ**

KUN readings
とも **tomo**

common words

友好　ゆうこう　**yūkō**　friendship
親友　しんゆう　**shin'yū**　close friend
友達　ともだち　**tomodachi**　friend
友情　ゆうじょう　**yūjō**　friendship
友人　ゆうじん　**yūjin**　friend
学友　がくゆう　**gakuyū**　school friend
校友　こうゆう　**kōyū**　schoolmate

人 (2 strokes)	meaning person radical 人(イ)	ON readings ジン **JIN,** ニン **NIN** KUN readings ひと **hito**	common words アメリカ人　アメリカじん **amerikajin** American (person) カナダ人　カナダじん **kanadajin** Canadian (person) イギリス人　イギリスじん **igirisujin** English (person) 大人　おとな **otona** adult 人生　じんせい **jinsei** human life 人体　じんたい **jintai** human body

手 (4 strokes)	meaning hand radical 手	ON readings シュ **SHU** KUN readings て **te**	common words 上手　じょうず **jōzu** good at something 下手　へた **heta** not good at something 手分けをする　てわけをする **tewake o suru** to divide up work 人手　ひとで **hitode** other people; other people's assistance; workers 手を入れる　てをいれる **te o ireru** to repair

目 (5 strokes)	meaning	ON readings	common words
	eye	モク **MOKU**, ボク **BOKU**	目下　めした　**meshita**　one's subordinate 目上　めうえ　**meue**　one's superior 目次　もくじ　**mokuji**　table of contents 目的　もくてき　**mokuteki**　purpose 一目　ひとめ　**hitome**　a glimpse, glance 目つき　めつき　**metsuki**　the look in one's eyes 目につく　めにつく　**me ni tsuku**　to catch one's eye
	radical 目	KUN readings め **me**, ま **ma**	

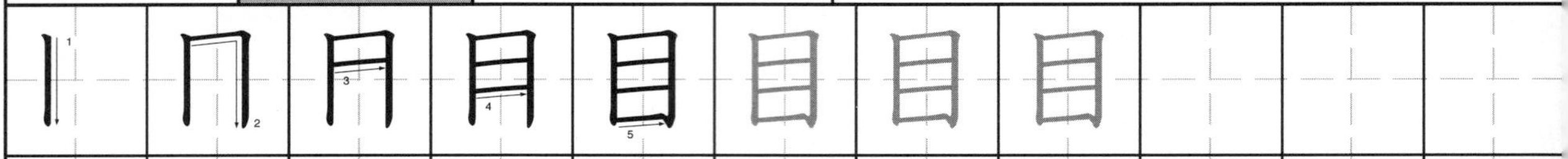

足 (7 strokes)	meaning	ON readings	common words
	foot, leg	ソク **SOKU**	不足　ふそく　**fusoku**　insufficiency 一足　いっそく　**issoku**　a pair (of shoes) 手足　てあし　**teashi**　arms and legs 足下　あしもと　**ashimoto**　at one's feet (also written 足元) 足す　たす　**tasu**　to add 足りる　たりる　**tariru**　to be enough
	radical 足	KUN readings あし **ashi**, た-りる **ta-riru**, た-す **ta-su**	

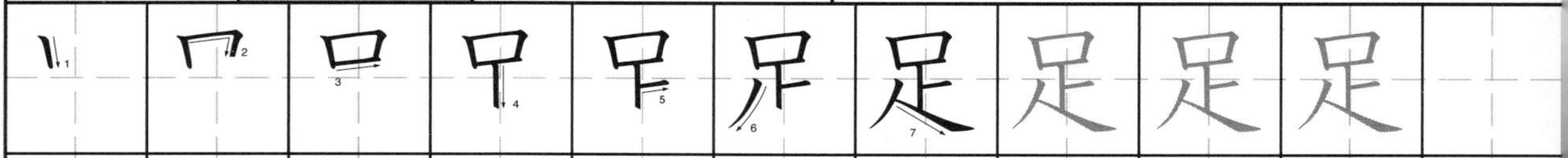

	meaning	ON readings	common words
# 耳 **(6 strokes)**	ear **radical** 耳	ジ **JI** **KUN readings** みみ **mimi**	耳が聞こえない　みみがきこえない　**mimi ga kikoenai**　deaf 耳あて　みみあて　**mimiate**　earmuffs 耳から学ぶ　みみからまなぶ　**mimi kara manabu**　to learn by ear 耳たぶ　みみたぶ　**mimitabu**　earlobe 耳に入る　みみに入る　**mimi ni hairu**　to happen to hear

	meaning	ON readings	common words
# 口 **(3 strokes)**	mouth **radical** 口	コウ **KŌ**, ク **KU** **KUN readings** くち **kuchi**	入口　いりぐち　**iriguchi**　entrance 人口　じんこう　**jinkō**　population 出口　でぐち　**deguchi**　exit 口座　こうざ　**kōza**　bank account 窓口　まどぐち　**madoguchi**　ticket window 一口　ひとくち　**hitokuchi**　a mouthful, a bite 口調　くちょう　**kuchō**　(oratorial) tone

左

(5 strokes)

meaning
left

radical
工

ON readings
サ **SA**

KUN readings
ひだり **hidari**

common words

左側　ひだりがわ　**hidarigawa**　left side
左利き(の)　ひだりきき(の)　**hidarikiki (no)**　left handed
左手　ひだりて　**hidarite**　left hand
左右　さゆう　**sayū**　left and right
左クリック　ひだりクリック　**hidari kurikku**　left click (on a mouse)

右

(5 strokes)

meaning
right

radical
口

ON readings
ウ **U**, ユウ **YŪ**

KUN readings
みぎ **migi**

common words

右側　みぎがわ　**migigawa**　right side
右手　みぎて　**migite**　right hand
右腕　みぎうで　**migiude**　right-hand man
右ハンドル　みぎハンドル　**migi handoru**　right-hand drive (car)
右カーブ　みぎカーブ　**migi kābu**　right-hand bend in the road

前 (9 strokes)	meaning	ON readings	common words
	before, in front of, previous **radical** 刂	ゼン **ZEN** **KUN readings** まえ **mae**	前後　ぜんご　**zengo**　before and after 〜年(日)前　〜ねん(にち)まえ　**... nen(nichi)mae** … years (days) ago 前半　ぜんはん/ぜんぱん　**zenhan/zenpan** first half 前日　ぜんじつ　**zenjitsu**　the previous day 以前の　いぜんの　**izen no**　former, previous

後 (9 strokes)	meaning	ON readings	common words
	behind; after; the remainder **radical** 彳	ゴ **GO**, コウ **KŌ** **KUN readings** うし-ろ **ushi-ro**, のち **nochi**, あと **ato,** おく-れる **oku-reru**,	後半　こうはん　**kōhan**　second half 食後　しょくご　**shokugo**　after a meal 〜年(日)後　〜ねん(にち)ご　**... nen(nichi)go** … years (days) after 以後　いご　**igo**　afterward 後ろ　うしろ　**ushiro**　behind 後日　ごじつ　**gojitsu**　at a later date, future 後で　あとで　**ato de**　later, afterward

上

(3 strokes)

meaning
top; above; on; upper

radical
一

ON readings
ジョウ **JŌ**, ショウ **SHŌ**

KUN readings
うえ **ue**, あ-げる **a-geru**, あ-がる **a-garu**, の-ぼる **no-boru**, うわ **uwa**, かみ **kami**

common words

屋上	おくじょう	**okujō**	roof
上がる	あがる	**agaru**	to rise
上げる	あげる	**ageru**	to raise
上ぼる	のぼる	**noboru**	to go up
上り坂	のぼりざか	**noborizaka**	uphill slope
上着	うわぎ	**uwagi**	overcoat

下

(3 strokes)

meaning
bottom; under; base; lower

radical
一

ON readings
ゲ **GE**, カ **KA**

KUN readings
した**shita**, しも**shimo**, もと**moto**, さ-げる**sa-geru**, さ-がる**sa-garu**, くだ-る**kuda-ru**, くだ-す**kuda-su**, くだ-さる**kuda-saru**, お-りる**o-riru**

common words

下る	くだる	**kudaru**	to go down
下さい	ください	**kudasai**	please give it to me
靴下	くつした	**kutsushita**	socks
地下鉄	ちかてつ	**chikatetsu**	subway
下りる	おりる	**oriru**	to go down; to get off
下がる	さがる	**sagaru**	to hang down, to go down
下目	したため	**shitame**	downward glance

中

(4 strokes)

meaning
middle; within; inside

radical
丨

ON readings
チュウ **CHŪ**

KUN readings
なか **naka**

common words

一日中	いちにちじゅう	**ichinichijū**	all day long
使用中	しようちゅう	**shiyōchū**	in use, occupied
中古	ちゅうこ	**chūko**	used, secondhand
集中する	しゅうちゅうする	**shūchū suru**	to concentrate
中学校	ちゅうがっこう	**chūgakkō**	junior high school
中国	ちゅうごく	**chūgoku**	China
中間	ちゅうかん	**chūkan**	the middle; intermediate

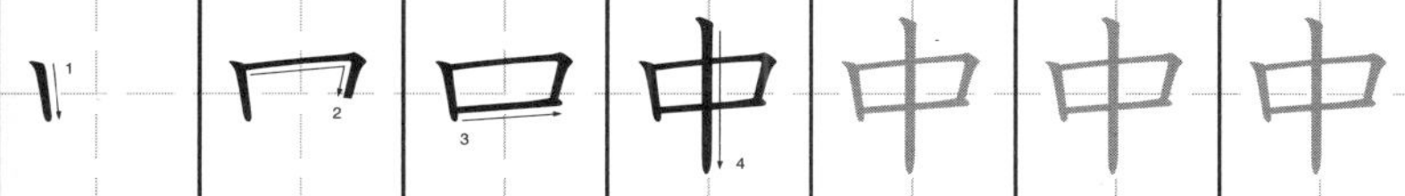

外

(5 strokes)

meaning
outside; foreign; other

radical
夕

ON readings
ガイ **GAI**, ゲ **GE**

KUN readings
そと **soto**, ほか **hoka**,
はず-す **hazu-su**,
はず-れる **hazu-reru**

common words

外出する	がいしゅつする	**gaishutsu suru**	to go out
外国人	がいこくじん	**gaikokujin**	foreigner
外側	そとがわ	**sotogawa**	outside
野外	やがい	**yagai**	outdoors
外れる	はずれる	**hazureru**	to come off, slip
案外	あんがい	**angai**	unexpectedly

北

(5 strokes)

meaning
north

radical
匕

ON readings
ホク **HOKU**

KUN readings
きた **kita**

common words

東北地方　とうほくちほう　**Tōhoku chihō**　Tohoku district
北部　ほくぶ　**hokubu**　northern district/part
北口　きたぐち　**kitaguchi**　north exit
北国　きたぐに　**kitaguni**　northern country
北アメリカ　きたアメリカ　**kita amerika**　North America
北海道　ほっかいどう　**Hokkaidō**　Hokkaido

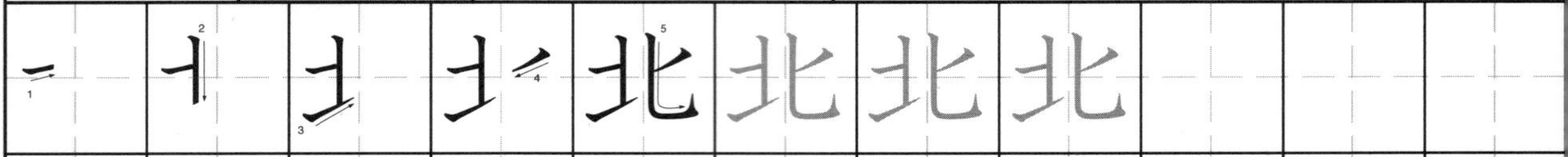

南

(9 strokes)

meaning
south

radical
十

ON readings
ナン **NAN**

KUN readings
みなみ **minami**

common words

南口　みなみぐち　**minamiguchi**　south exit
東南アジア　とうなんアジア　**tōnan ajia**　Southeast Asia
南アメリカ　みなみアメリカ　**minami amerika**　South America
南アフリカ　みなみアフリカ　**minami afurika**　South Africa
南国　なんごく　**nangoku**　southern country
南西　なんせい　**nansei**　southwest

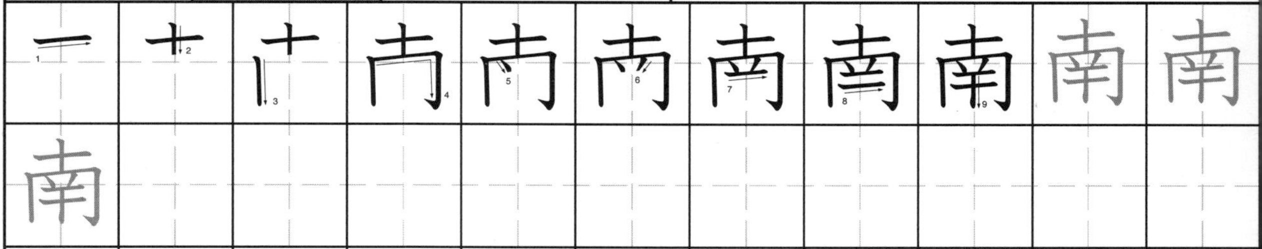

東

(8 strokes)

meaning
east

radical
木

ON readings
トウ **TŌ**

KUN readings
ひがし **higashi**

common words
中東　ちゅうとう **chūtō** the Middle East
東西南北　とうざいなんぼく **tōzainanboku** north,south, east, and west
東ヨーロッパ　ひがしヨーロッパ **higashi yōroppa** Eastern Europe
東西　とうざい **tōzai** east and west
東口　ひがしぐち **higashiguchi** east exit

西

(6 strokes)

meaning
west

radical
西

ON readings
セイ **SEI**, サイ **SAI**

KUN readings
にし **nishi**

common words
西部　せいぶ **seibu** western district/part
西口　にしぐち **nishiguchi** west exit
北西　ほくせい **hokusei** northwest
古今東西　ここんとうざい **kokontōzai** all times and places
西ヨーロッパ　にしヨーロッパ **nishi yōroppa** Western Europe

白 (5 strokes)	meaning: white radical: 白	ON readings: ハク **HAKU**, ビャク **BYAKU** KUN readings: しろ **shiro**, しろ-い **shiro-i**, しら **shira**	common words: 白い しろい **shiroi** white 面白い おもしろい **omoshiroi** interesting 空白 くうはく **kūhaku** blank 白ワイン しろワイン **shirowain** white wine 白紙 はくし **hakushi** blank paper 白人 はくじん **hakujin** white person 白日 はくじつ **hakujitsu** broad daylight

花 (7 strokes)	meaning: flower radical: 艹	ON readings: カ **KA** KUN readings: はな **hana**	common words: 花びん かびん **kabin** vase 生け花 いけばな **ikebana** ikebana (Japanese flower arranging) 花たば はなたば **hanataba** bouquet 花見 はなみ **hanami** cherry blossom viewing 国花 こっか **kokka** national flower

川 (3 strokes)	meaning: river, stream	ON readings: セン **SEN**	common words
	radical: 川	KUN readings: かわ **kawa**	河川 かせん **kasen** river, stream 川辺 かわべ **kawabe** riverside 川上 かわかみ **kawakami** upriver 小川 おがわ **ogawa** stream 川下 かわしも **kawashimo** downstream

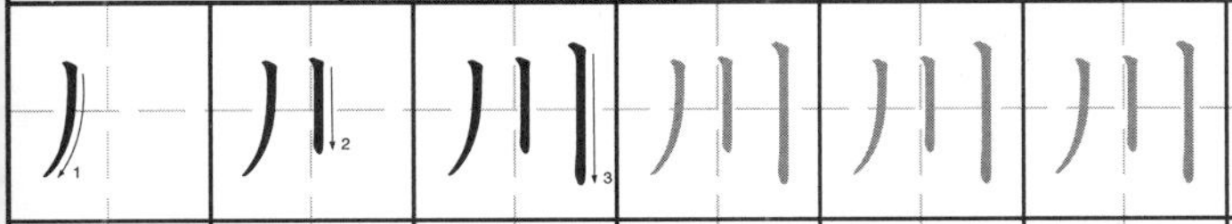

山 (3 strokes)	meaning: mountain	ON readings: サン **SAN**	common words
	radical: 山	KUN readings: やま **yama**	山のぼり やまのぼり **yamanobori** mountain climbing 山道 やまみち **yamamichi** mountain road 氷山 ひょうざん **hyōzan** iceberg 富士山 ふじさん **Fuji-san** Mount Fuji

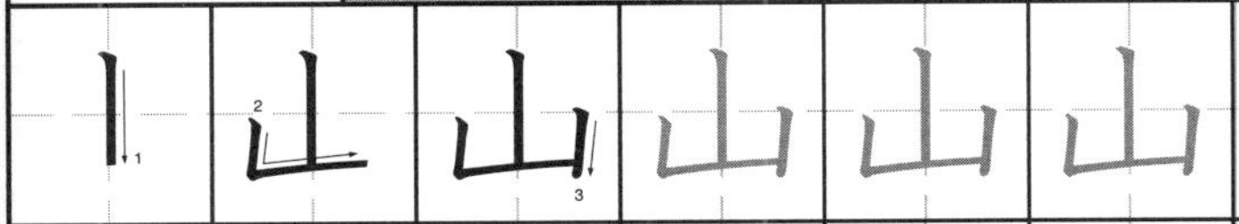

空 (8 strokes)	meaning sky; vacancy; emptiness radical 穴	ON readings クウ **KŪ** KUN readings そら **sora**, あ-く **a-ku**, あ-ける **a-keru**, から **kara**	common words 空気　くうき **kūki** air 空っぽ　からっぽ **karappo** empty 空手　からて **karate** karate 航空便　こうくうびん **kōkūbin** airmail 空く　あく **aku** to become empty 空ける　あける **akeru** to vacate

天 (4 strokes)	meaning sky, heaven radical 大	ON readings テン **TEN** KUN readings あめ **ame**, あま **ama**	common words 天の川　あまのがわ **amanogawa** the Milky Way 天然　てんねん **ten'nen** nature 天気予報　てんきよほう **tenkiyohō** weather forecast 天国　てんごく **tengoku** paradise, heaven 天気　てんき **tenki** weather 天使　てんし **tenshi** angel

気 (6 strokes)	meaning	ON readings	common words
	spirit, energy, mind	キ **KI**, ケ **KE**	気分　きぶん　**kibun**　feeling 気が小さい　きがちいさい　**ki ga chīsai**　nervous, timid 気になる　きになる　**ki ni naru**　to be worried about 気がつく　きがつく　**ki ga tsuku**　to notice 人気　にんき　**ninki**　popularity 電気　でんき　**denki**　electricity
	radical 气	KUN readings	

雨 (8 strokes)	meaning	ON readings	common words
	rain	ウ **U**	雨ふり　あめふり　**amefuri**　rainy weather 小雨　こさめ　**kosame**　drizzle 雨期　うき　**uki**　rainy season 雨天　うてん　**uten**　rainy weather 大雨　おおあめ　**ōame**　heavy rain 梅雨　つゆ　**tsuyu**　rainy season 雨水　あまみず　**amamizu**　rainwater
	radical 雨	KUN readings あめ **ame**, あま **ama**	

学

(8 strokes)

meaning
learning, studies

radical
子

ON readings
ガク **GAKU**

KUN readings
まな-ぶ **mana-bu**

common words
学ぶ　まなぶ　**manabu**　to study, to learn
学食　がくしょく　**gakushoku**　school cafeteria
大学　だいがく　**daigaku**　university
学習する　がくしゅうする　**gakushū suru**　to learn, to study
学生　がくせい　**gakusei**　student
学内　がくない　**gakunai**　within the school
電子学　でんしがく　**denshigaku**　electronics (study)

校

(10 strokes)

meaning
school

radical
木

ON readings
コウ **KŌ**

KUN readings

common words
学校　がっこう　**gakkō**　school
小学校　しょうがっこう　**shōgakkō**　elementary school
校長　こうちょう　**kōchō**　school principal
高校　こうこう　**kōkō**　high school
校舎　こうしゃ　**kōsha**　school building
母校　ぼこう　**bokō**　alma mater
校門　こうもん　**kōmon**　school gate

先

(6 strokes)

meaning
future; ahead; point; tip

radical
儿

ON readings
セン **SEN**

KUN readings
さき **saki**

common words

先生　せんせい　**sensei**　teacher
あて先　あてさき　**atesaki**　(destination) address
先払い　さきばらい　**sakibarai**　advance payment
先日　せんじつ　**senjitsu**　the other day
つま先　つまさき　**tsumasaki**　tip of the toe
指先　ゆびさき　**yubisaki**　fingertip
優先　ゆうせん　**yūsen**　priority, precedence

1 2 3 4 5 6

先 先 先

生

(5 strokes)

meaning
birth; life

radical
生

ON readings
セイ **SEI**, ショウ **SHŌ**

KUN readings
い-きる **i-kiru,** い-かす **i-kasu,** い-ける **i-keru,** う-まれる **u-mareru,** う-む **u-mu,** お-う **o-u,** は-える **ha-eru,** は-やす **ha-yasu,** き **ki,** なま **nama**

common words

生まれる　うまれる　**umareru**　to be born
生きる　いきる　**ikiru** to live
生徒　せいと　**seito**　student
生活　せいかつ　**seikatsu**　life; living
生ビール　なまビール　**nama bīru**　draft beer
生ゴミ　なまゴミ　**nama gomi**　kitchen garbage

1 2 3 4 5

生 生 生

体

(7 strokes)

meaning
body

radical
亻

ON readings
タイ **TAI**, テイ **TEI**

KUN readings
からだ **karada**

common words

気体	きたい	**kitai**	gas, vapor
体験	たいけん	**taiken**	experience
本体	ほんたい	**hontai**	body (of a machine)
大体	だいたい	**daitai**	more or less, just about
車体	しゃたい	**shatai**	body of a car
体内	たいない	**tainai**	inside the body
体裁	ていさい	**teisai**	appearance

本

(5 strokes)

meaning
book; main; true; counter for long objects

radical
木

ON readings
ホン **HON**

KUN readings
もと **moto**

common words

本名	ほんみょう	**honmyō**	real name
本人	ほんにん	**hon'nin**	the person him/herself
本年	ほんねん	**hon'nen**	this year (formal)
本日	ほんじつ	**honjitsu**	today (formal)
手本	てほん	**tehon**	model, good example
日本人	にほんじん	**Nihonjin**	Japanese person
本気で	ほんきで	**honki de**	seriously

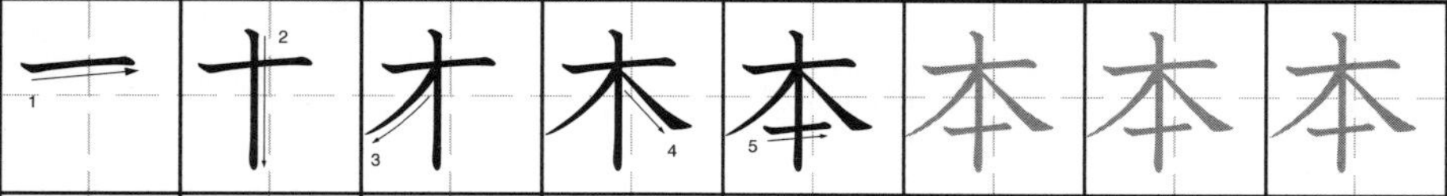

書

(10 strokes)

meaning
calligraphy; book; letter

radical
日

ON readings
ショ **SHO**

KUN readings
か-く **ka-ku**

common words
書く　かく　**kaku**　to write
図書館　としょかん　**toshokan**　library
辞書　じしょ　**jisho**　dictionary
秘書　ひしょ　**hisho**　secretary
書類　しょるい　**shorui**　documents
書体　しょたい　**shotai**　font, character style
書道　しょどう　**shodō**　calligraphy

読

(14 strokes)

meaning
to read

radical
言

ON readings
ドク **DOKU,** トク **TOKU,** トウ **TŌ**

KUN readings
よ-む **yo-mu**

common words
読む　よむ　**yomu**　to read
読書　どくしょ　**dokusho**　reading
読書会　どくしょかい　**dokushokai**　reading circle
音読み　おんよみ　**on'yomi**　Chinese-style reading of a character
訓読み　くんよみ　**kun'yomi**　Japanese-style reading of a character

見 (7 strokes)	meaning to see, to look radical 見	ON readings ケン **KEN** KUN readings み-る **mi-ru,** み-える **mi-eru,** み-せる **mi-seru**	common words 見せる　みせる　**miseru**　to show, to display 意見　いけん　**iken**　opinion 見学する　けんがくする　**kengaku suru**　to observe (for learning) 発見　はっけん　**hakken**　discovery 会見　かいけん　**kaiken**　interview 見出し　みだし　**midashi**　headline, heading

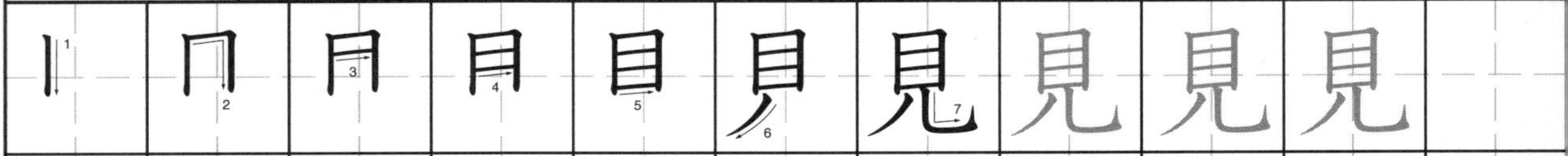

聞 (14 strokes)	meaning to hear; to listen to; to obey; to ask radical 耳	ON readings ブン **BUN,** モン **MON** KUN readings き-く **ki-ku,** き-こえる **ki-koeru**	common words 聞く　きく　**kiku**　to listen; ask 聞き手　ききて　**kikite**　listener 聞き入れる　ききいれる　**kikiireru**　to comply with 聞き上手な　ききじょうずな　**kikijōzuna**　good listener 前代未聞の　ぜんだいみもんの　**zendaimimon no** unprecedented 見聞きする　みききする　**mikiki suru**　to see and hear

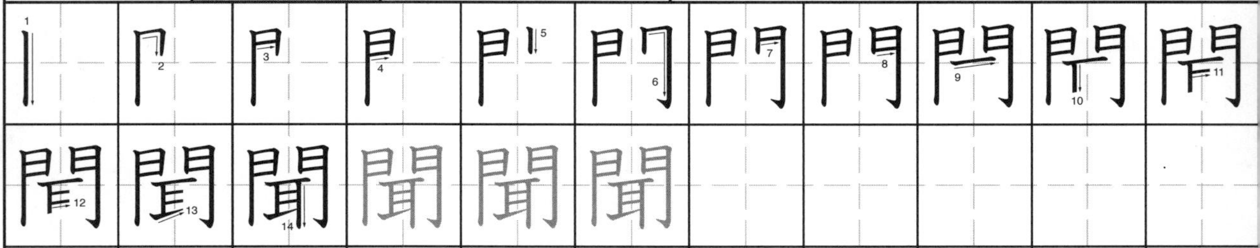

言 (7 strokes)	meaning: speech; statement; to say radical: 言	ON readings: ゲン GEN, ゴン GON KUN readings: い-う i-u, こと koto	common words

common words

言う　いう　**iu**　to say
言い訳　いいわけ　**iiwake**　excuse
方言　ほうげん　**hōgen**　dialect
無言　むごん　**mugon**　silence
言葉　ことば　**kotoba**　word, language

1 2 3 4 5 6 7

語 (14 strokes)	meaning: word; language radical: 言	ON readings: ゴ GO KUN readings: かた-らう kata-rau, かた-る kata-ru	common words

common words

語る　かたる　**kataru**　to tell; to talk
小言を言う　こごとをいう　**kogoto o iu**　to scold
語学　ごがく　**gogaku**　language study
言語　げんご　**gengo**　language, speech
外来語　がいらいご　**garaigo**　loanword
語り手　かたりて　**katarite**　narrator
中国語　ちゅうごくご　**chūgokugo**　Chinese language

1 2 3 4 5 6 7 8 9 10 11 12 13 14

車

(7 strokes)

meaning	ON readings	common words
wheel, vehicle, car	シャ **SHA**	新車　しんしゃ　**shinsha** new car 下車する　げしゃする　**gesha suru** to get off (a bus, train) 車内　しゃない　**shanai** inside of a car/train 電車　でんしゃ　**densha** train 車道　しゃどう　**shadō** road for cars 自転車　じてんしゃ　**jitensha** bicycle 中古車　ちゅうこしゃ　**chūkosha** secondhand car
radical 車	**KUN readings** くるま **kuruma**	

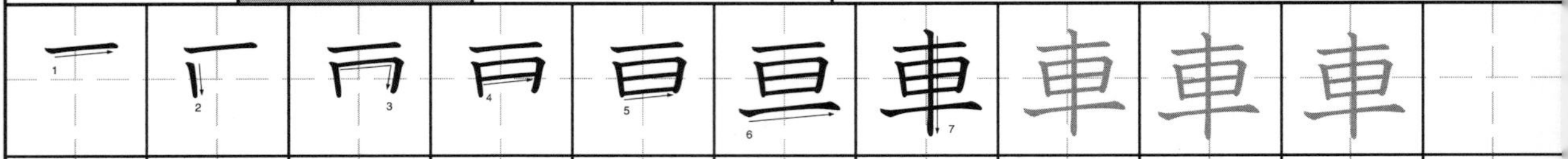

駅

(14 strokes)

meaning	ON readings	common words
station	エキ **EKI**	駅員　えきいん　**eki'in** station staff 駅弁　えきべん　**ekiben** station bento box 駅長　えきちょう　**ekichō** station master 駅前　えきまえ　**ekimae** in front of the station 駅ビル　えきビル　**eki biru** station building
radical 馬	**KUN readings**	

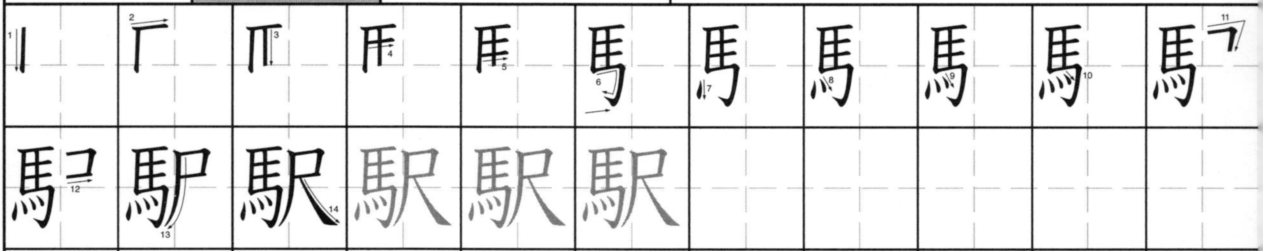

会 (6 strokes)	**meaning** meeting; party; society; to see; to meet **radical** 𠆢	**ON readings** カイ **KAI,** エ **E** **KUN readings** あ-う **a-u**	**common words**
			集会 しゅうかい **shūkai** meeting, assembly 会社 かいしゃ **kaisha** company 社会人 しゃかいじん **shakaijin** member of society 会計学 かいけいがく **kaikeigaku** accounting (study) 電気会社 でんきがいしゃ **denki gaisha** electric company 会計 かいけい **kaikei** bill, accounts

社 (7 strokes)	**meaning** company, firm, corporation; shrine **radical** 示（ネ）	**ON readings** シャ **SHA** **KUN readings** やしろ **yashiro**	**common words**
			社長 しゃちょう **shachō** president 社会 しゃかい **shakai** society; community 神社 じんじゃ **jinja** Shinto shrine 本社 ほんしゃ **honsha** head office 社内 しゃない **shanai** inside the company 社名 しゃめい **shamei** company name

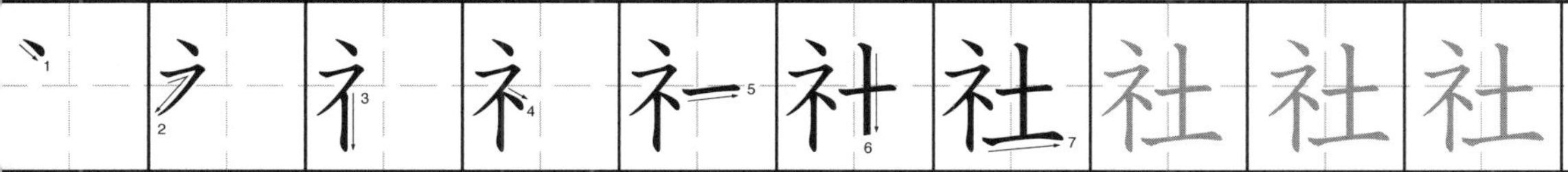

行

(6 strokes)

meaning
to go; proceed; conduct

radical
行

ON readings
コウ **KŌ,** ギョウ **GYŌ,** アン **AN**

KUN readings
い-く **i-ku,** おこな-う **okona-u,** ゆ-く **yu-ku**

common words
行く　いく　**iku**　to go
銀行　ぎんこう　**ginkō**　bank
飛行機　ひこうき　**hikōki**　airplane
旅行　りょこう　**ryokō**　trip, travel
行き会う　いきあう　**ikiau**　to meet by chance
行う　おこなう　**okonau**　to perform, to carry out
行き先　いきさき　**ikisaki**　destination

来

(7 strokes)

meaning
to come; since; next

radical
木

ON readings
ライ **RAI**

KUN readings
く-る **ku-ru,** き-たる **ki-taru,** き-たす **ki-tasu**

common words
来る　くる　**kuru**　to come
未来　みらい　**mirai**　future
将来　しょうらい　**shōrai**　future; prospects
出来上がる　できあがる　**dekiagaru**　to be completed
出来る　できる　**dekiru**　to be able to
来日する　らいにちする　**rainichi suru**　to come to Japan

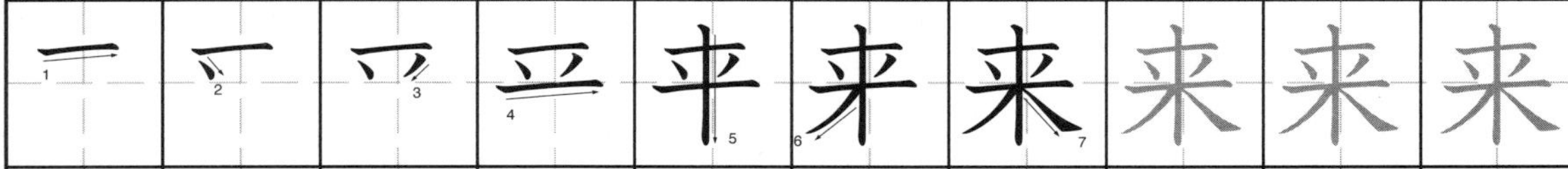

出 (5 strokes)	meaning	ON readings	common words
	to come out; to go out **radical** 凵	シュツ **SHUTSU,** スイ **SUI** **KUN readings** で-る **de-ru,** だ-す **da-su**	出入り口　でいりぐち **deiriguchi** entrance and exit 出かける　でかける **dekakeru** to go out 思い出　おもいで **omoide** memory 出国　しゅっこく **shukkoku** departure from a country 出席する　しゅっせきする **shusseki suru** to attend 出発　しゅっぱつ **shuppatsu** departure

入 (2 strokes)	meaning	ON readings	common words
	entering; attendance **radical** 入	ニュウ **NYŪ** **KUN readings** い-る **i-ru,** い-れる **i-reru,** はい-る **hai-ru**	入学する　にゅうがくする **nyūgaku suru** to be admitted to a school 入国　にゅうこく **nyūkoku** entry into a country (immigration) 収入　しゅうにゅう **shūnyū** earnings 入会する　にゅうかいする **nyūkai suru** to become a member of, enroll

国

(8 strokes)

meaning
country

radical
囗

ON readings
コク **KOKU**

KUN readings
くに **kuni**

common words
外国　がいこく **gaikoku** foreign country
国土　こくど **kokudo** country, territory
国外　こくがい **kokugai** overseas, abroad
国名　こくめい **kokumei** country name
国内　こくない **kokunai** domestic
国立大学　こくりつだいがく **kokuritsu daigaku** a national university

道

(12 strokes)

meaning
road, street, avenue, boulevard, path, way, course

radical
辶

ON readings
ドウ **DŌ,** トウ **TŌ**

KUN readings
みち **michi**

common words
片道　かたみち **katamichi** one way trip
国道　こくどう **kokudō** national highway
小道　こみち **komichi** lane, path
鉄道　てつどう **tetsudō** railway
道学　どうがく **dōgaku** Confucianism
神道　しんとう **shintō** Shinto, Shintoism

安

(6 strokes)

meaning
cheap, inexpensive; secure; to feel relieved

radical
宀

ON readings
アン **AN**

KUN readings
やすーい **yasu-i**

common words
安らかな　やすらかな　**yasurakana** untroubled, at ease
不安　ふあん　**fuan** anxiety
安っぽい　やすっぽい　**yasuppoi** cheap looking
安くする　やすくする　**yasuku suru** to knock the price down
ドル高　ドルだか　**dorudaka** a rise in value of the dollar
ドル安　ドルやす　**doruyasu** a drop in value of the dollar

高

(10 strokes)

meaning
high; expensive

radical
高

ON readings
コウ **KŌ**

KUN readings
たかーい **taka-i,** たか **taka,** たかーまる **taka-maru,** たかーめる **taka-meru**

common words
高級な　こうきゅうな　**kōkyū na** high-quality, luxury
高山　こうざん　**kōzan** high mountain
最高の　さいこうの　**saikō no** highest, maximum, best
名高い　なだかい　**nadakai** renowned
高さ　たかさ　**takasa** height
高名　こうめい　**kōmei** fame

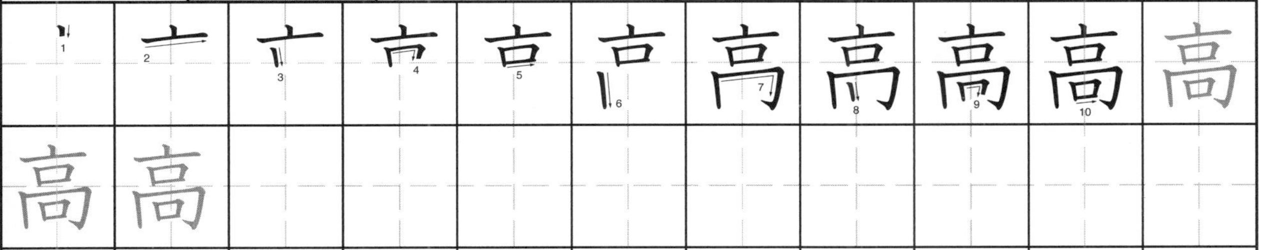

飲

(12 strokes)

meaning
drink

radical
食

ON readings
イン **IN,** オン **ON**

KUN readings
の－む **no-mu,**
の－み **no-mi**

common words

飲む　のむ　**nomu**　to drink
一飲み　ひとのみ　**hitonomi**　sip
飲みもの　のみもの　**nomimono**　beverage
飲食　いんしょく　**inshoku**　eating and drinking
飲みに行く　のみにいく　**nomi ni iku**　to go drinking
飲み水　のみみず　**nomimizu**　drinking water

食

(9 strokes)

meaning
food; to eat

radical
食

ON readings
ショク **SHOKU,** ジキ **JIKI**

KUN readings
く－う **ku-u,** く－らう **ku-rau,**
た－べる **ta-beru**

common words

食べる　たべる　**taberu**　to eat
外食　がいしょく　**gaishoku**　eating out
食事　しょくじ　**shokuji**　meal
食欲　しょくよく　**shokuyoku**　appetite
食べもの　たべもの　**tabemono**　food
食道　しょくどう　**shokudō**　esophagus
食前　しょくぜん　**shokuzen**　before meals

魚

(11 strokes)

meaning	ON readings	common words
fish	ギョ **GYO**	魚河岸　うおがし　**uogashi**　riverside fish market
	KUN readings	金魚　きんぎょ　**kingyo**　goldfish
radical	うお **uo,** さかな **sakana**	小魚　こざかな　**kozakana**　small fish
魚		人魚　にんぎょ　**ningyo**　mermaid
		魚屋　さかなや　**sakanaya**　fish shop

長

(8 strokes)

meaning	ON readings	common words
long; a chief	チョウ **CHŌ**	会長　かいちょう　**kaichō**　chairperson
	KUN readings	市長　しちょう　**shichō**　mayor
radical	なが-い **naga-i**	身長　しんちょう　**shinchō**　height
長		長さ　ながさ　**nagasa**　length
		学長　がくちょう　**gakuchō**　university president
		長女　ちょうじょ　**chōjo**　eldest daugher

古	meaning	ON readings	common words
(5 strokes)	old, ancient **radical** ロ	コ **KO** **KUN readings** ふる-い **furu-i**, ふる-す **furu-su**	古い ふるい **furui** old お古 おふる **ofuru** hand-me-downs 古代 こだい **kodai** ancient times, antiquity 古典 こてん **koten** classic 最古の さいこの **saiko no** the oldest 古本 ふるほん **furuhon** secondhand (used) book

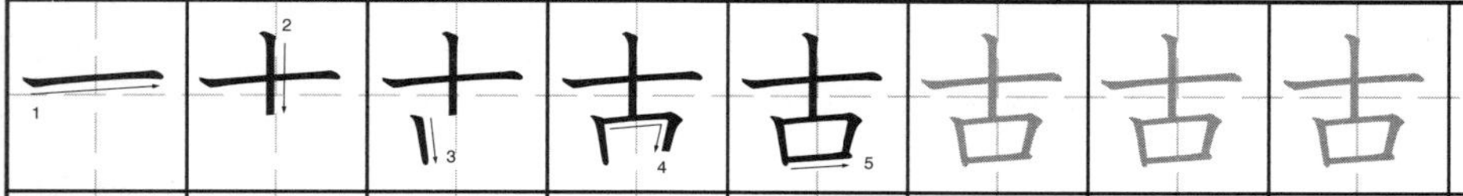

新	meaning	ON readings	common words
(13 strokes)	new, fresh, latest **radical** 斤	シン **SHINI** **KUN readings** あたら-しい **atara-shii**, あら-た **ara-ta,** にい **nii**	新しい あたらしい **atarashii** new 新人 しんじん **shinjin** newcomer 新品 しんぴん **shinpin** new [brand-new] article 新聞 しんぶん **shinbun** newspaper 新年 しんねん **shin'nen** the New Year 新入生 しんにゅうせい **shin'nyūsei** new student

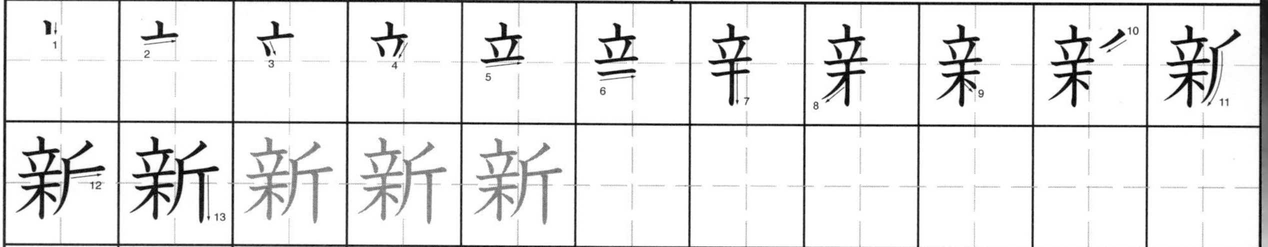

小	meaning	ON readings	common words
(3 strokes)	small; little	シ ョ ウ **SHŌ**	小さい　ちいさい　**chīsai**　small 小づかい　こづかい　**kozukai**　pocket money 小指　こゆび　**koyubi**　pinkie (finger) 小学生　しょうがくせい　**shōgakusei**　elementary school student 小説　しょうせつ　**shōsetsu**　novel; fiction 小エビ　こエビ　**ko ebi**　shrimp (small)
	radical 小	KUN readings ち い-さ い **chī-sai,** お- **o-,** こ- **ko-**	

大	meaning	ON readings	common words
(3 strokes)	big; large; great	ダイ **DAI,** タイ **TAI**	大きい　おおきい　**ōkii**　big 大好き　だいすき　**daisuki**　very fond of 大切　たいせつ　**taisetsu**　important 大急ぎで　おおいそぎで　**ōisogi de**　in a hurry; rushed 大小　だいしょう　**daishō**　large and small 大川　おおかわ　**ōkawa**　large river 大会　たいかい　**taikai**　convention, mass meeting
	radical 大	KUN readings おお- **ō-,** おお-きい **ō-kii,** おお-いに **ō-ini**	

少 (4 strokes)	**meaning** few; little **radical** 小	**ON readings** ショウ **SHŌ** **KUN readings** すく-ない **suku-nai,** すこ-し **suko-shi**	**common words** 少し　すこし　**sukoshi** a little 少年少女　しょうねんしょうじょ　**shōnen shōjo** boys and girls 少ない　すくない　**sukunai** few 少々　しょうしょう　**shōshō** a little; a few 少食　しょうしょく　**shōshoku** light eating 年少の　ねんしょうの　**nenshō** young, juvenile

多 (6 strokes)	**meaning** many; a lot; plenty of **radical** 夕	**ON readings** タ **TA** **KUN readings** おお-い **o'o-i**	**common words** 多い　おおい　**o'oi** many, numerous 多少　たしょう　**tashō** kind of, somewhat 多数の　たすうの　**tasū no** a lot of 大多数　だいたすう　**daitasū** large majority 多大な　ただいな　**tadai na** considerable, significant (amount)

買

(12 strokes)

meaning
to buy; to purchase

radical
貝

ON readings
バイ **BAI**

KUN readings
か-う **ka-u**

common words
買う　かう　**kau**　to buy
買い手　かいて　**kaite**　buyer
買いもの　かいもの　**kaimono**　shopping
買い得　かいどく　**kaidoku**　bargain
買い入れる　かいいれる　**kaiireru**　to purchase
買い足す　かいたす　**kaitasu**　to make additional purchases

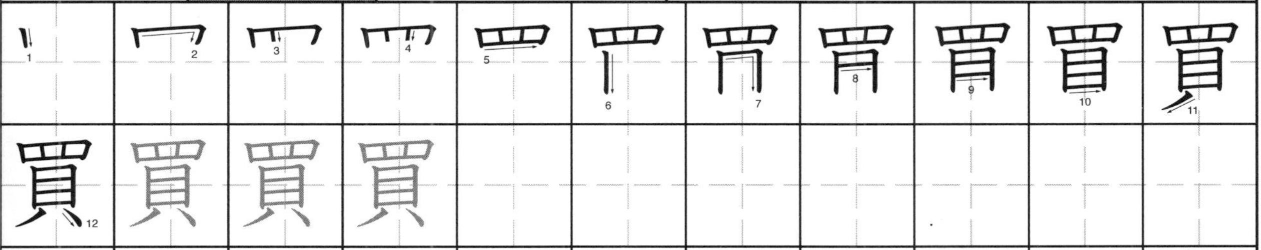

電

(13 strokes)

meaning
lightning; electricity

radical
雨

ON readings
デン **DEN**

KUN readings

common words
電気ショック　でんきショック　**denki shokku**　electric shock
電子　でんし　**denshi**　electron
電子タバコ　でんしタバコ　**denshi tabako**　electronic cigarette
電子レンジ　でんしレンジ　**denshi renji**　microwave oven

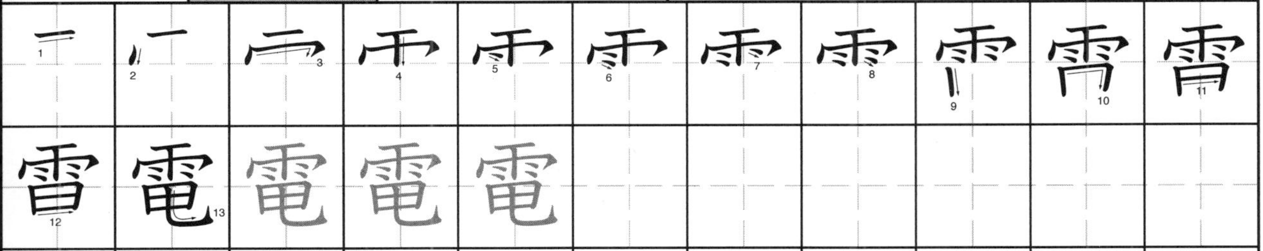

名 (6 strokes)	**meaning**	**ON readings**	**common words**
	name	メイ **MEI,** ミョウ **MYŌ**	名人　めいじん　**meijin**　expert 名前　なまえ　**namae**　name 名刺　めいし　**meishi**　business card 名言　めいげん　**meigen**　famous words 有名な　ゆうめいな　**yūmei na**　famous ファイル名　ファイルめい　**fairu mei** (computer) file name
	radical 口	**KUN readings** な **na**	

立 (6 strokes)	**meaning**	**ON readings**	**common words**
	to stand (up)	リツ **RITSU,** リュウ **RYŪ**	立つ　たつ　**tatsu**　to stand 立派な　りっぱな　**rippa na**　splendid 国立の　こくりつの　**kokuritsu no**　national 立体の　りったいの　**rittai no**　three-dimensional 立ち会い人　たちあいにん　**tachiainin**　witness 立ち上げる　たちあげる　**tachiageru**　to boot up (a computer)
	radical 立	**KUN readings** た-つ **ta-tsu,** た-てる **ta-teru**	

Writing Practice

PRACTICE 1
一 二 三 四 五

一つ　ひとつ　**hitotsu**　one (piece; age)

一	つ										

一月　いちがつ　**ichigatsu**　January

一	月										

二つ　ふたつ　**futatsu**　two (pieces; age)

二	つ										

二月　にがつ　**nigatsu**　February

二	月										

二人　ふたり　**futari**　two people

二	人										

二千　にせん　**nisen**　two thousand

二	千										

三つ　みっつ　**mittsu**　three (pieces; age)

三	つ										

三月　さんがつ　**sangatsu**　March

三	月										

三人　さんにん　**san'nin**　three people

三	人										

四つ　よっつ　**yottsu**　four (pieces; age)

四	つ										

四月　しがつ　**shigatsu**　April

四	月										

四人　よにん　**yonin**　four people

四	人										

四千　よんせん　**yonsen**　four thousand

四	千										

五つ　いつつ　**itsutsu**　five (pieces; age)

五	つ										

五月　ごがつ　**gogatsu**　May

五	月										

五十　ごじゅう　**gojū**　fifty

五	十										

五百　ごひゃく　**gohyaku**　five hundred

五	百										

五千　ごせん　**gosen**　five thousand

五	千										

PRACTICE 2
六 七 八 九

六つ　むっつ　**muttsu**　six (pieces; age)

六 つ

六月　ろくがつ　**rokugatsu**　June

六 月

六日　むいか　**muika**　six days; 6th of the month

六 日

六時　ろくじ　**rokuji**　six o'clock

六 時

七つ　ななつ　**nanatsu**　seven (pieces; age)

七 つ

七月　しちがつ　**shichigatsu**　July

七 月

七人　しちにん　**shichinin**　seven people

七 人

七百　ななひゃく　**nanahyaku**　seven hundred

七 百

七時　しちじ　**shichiji**　seven o'clock

七 時

八つ　やっつ　**yattsu**　eight (pieces; age)

八	つ										

八月　はちがつ　**hachigatsu**　August

八	月										

八日　ようか　**yōka**　eight days; 8th of the month

八	日										

八時　はちじ　**hachiji**　eight o'clock

八	時										

九つ　ここのつ　**kokonotsu**　nine (pieces; age)

九	つ										

九月　くがつ　**kugatsu**　September

九	月										

九人　きゅうにん　**kyūnin**　nine people

九	人										

九日　ここのか　**kokonoka**　nine days; 9th of the month

九	日										

九時　くじ　**kuji**　nine o'clock

九	時										

PRACTICE 3
十 百 千 万

十日　とおか　**tōka**　ten days; 10th of the month

十	日										

十万　じゅうまん　**jūman**　one hundred thousand

十	万										

十月　じゅうがつ　**jūgatsu**　October

十	月										

百人　ひゃくにん　**hyakunin**　one hundred people

百	人										

三百　さんびゃく　**sanbyaku**　three hundred

三	百										

五百　ごひゃく　**gohyaku**　five hundred

五	百										

百本　ひゃっぽん　**hyappon**　one hundred (trees, bottles, or long thing things)

百	本										

何百　なんびゃく　**nanbyaku**　how many hundreds

何	百										

千人　せんにん　**sen'nin**　one thousand people

千	人										

三千　さんぜん　**sanzen**　three thousand

三	千										

千円　せんえん　**sen'en**　one thousand yen

千	円										

十一月　じゅういちがつ　**jūichigatsu**　November

十	一	月									

十二月　じゅうにがつ　**jūnigatsu**　December

十	二	月									

二千円　にせんえん　**nisen'en**　two thousand yen

二	千	円									

五千円　ごせんえん　**gosen'en**　five thousand yen

五	千	円									

一万円　いちまんえん　**ichiman'en**　ten thousand yen

一	万	円									

一万人　いちまんにん　**ichiman'nin**　ten thousand people

一	万	人									

百万円　ひゃくまんえん　**hyakuman'en**　one million yen

百	万	円									

PRACTICE 4
円 曜 週 年

百円　ひゃくえん　**hyakuen**　one hundred yen

百	円										

円高　えんだか　**endaka**　high value of the yen

円	高										

円安　えんやす　**en'yasu**　low value of the yen

円	安										

今週　こんしゅう　**konshū**　this week

今	週										

週日　しゅうじつ　**shūjitsu**　weekday

週	日										

先週　せんしゅう　**senshū**　last week

先	週										

来週　らいしゅう　**raishū**　next week

来	週										

今年　ことし　**kotoshi**　this year

今	年										

毎年　まいねん　**mainen**　every year (can also be read as まいとし **maitoshi**)

毎	年										

年中　ねんじゅう　**nenjū**　throughout the year

年 中

毎週　まいしゅう　**maishū**　every week

毎 週

一年間　いちねんかん　**ichinenkan**　(a period of) one year

一 年 間

六年生　ろくねんせい　**rokunensei**　sixth grader

六 年 生

三週間　さんしゅうかん　**sanshūkan**　(a period of) three weeks

三 週 間

五年前　ごねんまえ　**gonenmae**　five years ago

五 年 前

月曜日　げつようび　**getsuyōbi**　Monday

月 曜 日

火曜日　かようび　**kayōbi**　Tuesday

火 曜 日

水曜日　すいようび　**suiyōbi**　Wednesday

水 曜 日

PRACTICE 5
日 月 火 水

一日 いちにち **ichinichi** one day (also read ついたち **tsuitachi** 1st of the month)

一	日										

二日 ふつか **futsuka** two days; 2nd of the month

二	日										

三日 みっか **mikka** three days; 3rd of the month

三	日										

日本 にほん **nihon** Japan (can also be read as にっぽん **nippon**)

日	本										

毎日 まいにち **mainichi** every day

毎	日										

今月 こんげつ **kongetsu** this month

今	月										

来月 らいげつ **raigetsu** next month

来	月										

先月 せんげつ **sengetsu** last month

先	月										

毎月 まいげつ **maigetsu** every month (can also be read as まいつき **maitsuki**)

毎	月										

火山　かざん **kazan** volcano

火	山										

花火　はなび **hanabi** fireworks

花	火										

火花　ひばな **hibana** spark

火	花										

お水　おみず **omizu** water

お	水										

水分　すいぶん **suibun** moisture

水	分										

二十日　はつか **hatsuka** 20th of the month

二	十	日									

日曜日　にちようび **nichiyōbi** Sunday

日	曜	日									

生年月日　せいねんがっぴ **seinengappi** date of birth

生	年	月	日								

日の出前　ひのでまえ **hinode mae** before sunrise

日	の	出	前								

PRACTICE 6
木 金 土 午

お金　おかね　**okane**　money

お	金										

前金　まえきん　**maekin**　advance (money)

前	金										

土間　どま　**doma**　dirt floor (in traditional house)

土	間										

金子　かねこ　**Kaneko**　Kaneko (Japanese surname)

金	子										

土手　どて　**dote**　embankment

土	手										

木曜日　もくようび　**mokuyōbi**　Thursday

木	曜	日									

金曜日　きんようび　**kinyōbi**　Friday

金	曜	日									

高い木　たかいき　**takai ki**　tall tree

高	い	木									

木の下　きのした　**ki no shita**　under a tree

木	の	下									

土と水　つちとみず　**tsuchi to mizu**　soil and water

土	と	水									

土足で　どそくで　**dosoku de**　with footwear on

土	足	で									

午前中　ごぜんちゅう　**gozenchū**　all morning

午	前	中									

土曜日　どようび　**doyōbi**　Saturday

土	曜	日									

午前一時　ごぜんいちじ　**gozen ichiji**　1 a.m.

午	前	一	時								

午前八時　ごぜんはちじ　**gozen hachiji**　8 a.m.

午	前	八	時								

午後二時　ごごにじ　**gogo niji**　2 p.m.

午	後	二	時								

午後六時　ごごろくじ　**gogo rokuji**　6 p.m.

午	後	六	時								

金メダル　きんメダル　**kinmedaru**　gold medal

金	メ	ダ	ル								

PRACTICE 7
今 分 半 毎

今日　きょう　**kyō**　today

今	日										

半月　はんつき　**hantsuki**　half a month　(can also be read as はんげつ **hangetsu**)

半	月										

七分　ななふん　**nanafun**　seven minutes

七	分										

半分　はんぶん　**hanbun**　half

半	分										

半年　はんとし　**hantoshi**　half a year

半	年										

毎時　まいじ　**maiji**　every hour

毎	時										

半日　はんにち　**han'nichi**　half a day

半	日										

五分　ごふん　**gofun**　five minutes

五	分										

半ば　なかば　**nakaba**　halfway

半	ば										

日毎に　ひごとに　**higoto ni**　daily

日	毎	に									

年毎に　としごとに　**toshigoto ni**　annually

年	毎	に									

三日分　みっかぶん　**mikkabun**　three days' worth

三	日	分									

分かる　わかる　**wakaru**　to understand

分	か	る									

分ける　わける　**wakeru**　to divide

分	け	る									

一時半　いちじはん　**ichijihan**　half past one

一	時	半									

今すぐ　いますぐ　**imasugu**　right now

今	す	ぐ									

半年毎に　はんとしごとに　**hantoshigoto ni**　bi-annually

半	年	毎	に								

三日毎に　みっかごとに　**mikkagoto ni**　every three days

三	日	毎	に								

PRACTICE 8
何 時 計 間

何月　なんがつ　**nangatsu**　what month

何	月										

何年　なんねん　**nan'nen**　what year; how many years

何	年										

何分　なんぷん　**nanpun**　how many minutes

何	分										

時間　じかん　**jikan**　time, hour

時	間										

日時　にちじ　**nichiji**　the date and time

日	時										

時計　とけい　**tokei**　watch; clock

時	計										

計る　はかる　**hakaru**　to measure

計	る										

何人　なんにん　**nan'nin**　how many people

何	人										

七時　しちじ　**shichiji**　seven o'clock

七	時										

何時　なんじ　**nanji**　what time

何	時										

人間　にんげん　**ningen**　human being

人	間										

何日間　なんにちかん　**nan'nichikan**　how many days

何	日	間									

何週間　なんしゅうかん　**nanshūkan**　how many weeks

何	週	間									

一時間　いちじかん　**ichijikan**　one hour

一	時	間									

時間外　じかんがい　**jikangai**　overtime

時	間	外									

年間の　ねんかんの　**nenkan no**　annual

年	間	の									

この間　このあいだ　**kono aida**　the other day

こ	の	間									

二日間　ふつかかん　**futsukakan**　for two days

二	日	間									

PRACTICE 9
男 女 父 母

男子　だんし　**danshi**　man, boy

男	子										

男女　だんじょ　**danjo**　men and women

男	女										

父上　ちちうえ　**chichiue**　father (archaic)

父	上										

父子　ふし　**fushi**　father and child

父	子										

父母　ふぼ　**fubo**　parents

父	母										

母上　ははうえ　**hahaue**　mother (archaic)

母	上										

女子　じょし　**joshi**　woman, girl

女	子										

母国　ぼこく　**bokoku**　mother country

母	国										

少女　しょうじょ　**shōjo**　girl

少	女										

長男　ちょうなん　**chōnan**　eldest son

長	男										

男の子　おとこのこ　**otoko no ko**　boy

男	の	子									

女の子　おんなのこ　**on'na no ko**　girl

女	の	子									

女子大　じょしだい　**joshidai**　women's university

女	子	大									

父の日　ちちのひ　**chichi no hi**　Father's Day

父	の	日									

母の日　ははのひ　**haha no hi**　Mother's Day

母	の	日									

男らしい　おとこらしい　**otoko rashii**　masculine

男	ら	し	い								

お父さん　おとうさん　**otōsan**　father

お	父	さ	ん								

お母さん　おかあさん　**okāsan**　mother

お	母	さ	ん								

PRACTICE 10
子 友 人 手

手足　てあし　**teashi**　arms and legs

手	足										

上手　じょうず　**jōzu**　good at something

上	手										

友子　ともこ　**Tomoko**　Tomoko (Japanese female given name)

友	子										

大人　おとな　**otona**　adult

大	人										

友人　ゆうじん　**yūjin**　friend

友	人										

下手　へた　**heta**　not good at something

下	手										

一人　ひとり　**hitori**　one person

一	人										

学友　がくゆう　**gakuyū**　school friend

学	友										

人生　じんせい　**jinsei**　human life

人	生										

人手　ひとで **hitode** other people; other people's assistance; workers

人	手										

手本　てほん **tehon** model, good example

手	本										

子会社　こがいしゃ **kogaisha** subsidiary company

子	会	社									

子ども　こども **kodomo** child

子	ど	も									

カナダ人　カナダじん **kanadajin** Canadian person

カ	ナ	ダ	人								

イギリス人　イギリスじん **igirisujin** English person

イ	ギ	リ	ス	人					

アメリカ人　アメリカじん **amerikajin** American

ア	メ	リ	カ	人					

手を入れる　てをいれる **te o ireru** to repair

手	を	入	れ	る					

手分けをする　てわけをする **tewake o suru** to divide up work

手	分	け	を	す	る						

PRACTICE 11
目 足 耳 口

出口　でぐち　**deguchi**　exit

出	口										

一足　いっそく　**issoku**　a pair (of shoes)

一	足										

目上　めうえ　**meue**　one's superior

目	上										

足下　あしもと　**ashimoto**　at one's feet

足	下										

足す　たす　**tasu**　to add

足	す										

目下　めした　**meshita**　one's subordinate

目	下										

一目　ひとめ　**hitome**　a glimpse, glance

一	目										

入口　いりぐち　**iriguchi**　entrance

入	口										

人口　じんこう　**jinkō**　population

人	口										

一口　ひとくち　**hitokuchi**　a mouthful, a bite

一 口

目つき　めつき　**metsuki**　the look in one's eyes

目 つ き

足りる　たりる　**tariru**　to be enough

足 り る

耳たぶ　みみたぶ　**mimitabu**　earlobe

耳 た ぶ

耳あて　みみあて　**mimiate**　ear muffs

耳 あ て

耳に入る　みみにはいる　**mimi ni hairu**　to happen to hear

耳 に 入 る

目につく　めにつく　**me ni tsuku**　to catch one's eye

目 に つ く

耳から学ぶ　みみからまなぶ　**mimi kara manabu**　to learn by ear

耳 か ら 学 ぶ

耳が聞こえない　みみがきこえない　**mimi ga kikoenai**　deaf

耳 が 聞 こ え な い

PRACTICE 12
右 左 前 後

前日　ぜんじつ　**zenjitsu**　the previous day

前	日										

午後　ごご　**gogo**　afternoon, p.m.

午	後										

後ろ　うしろ　**ushiro**　behind

後	ろ										

右手　みぎて　**migite**　right hand

右	手										

左手　ひだりて　**hidarite**　left hand

左	手										

左右　さゆう　**sayū**　left and right

左	右										

後半　こうはん　**kōhan**　second half

後	半										

前後　ぜんご　**zengo**　before and after

前	後										

前半　ぜんはん　**zenhan**　first half (can also be read as ぜんぱん **zenpan**)

前	半										

後で　あとで　**ato de**　later, afterward

後	で										

後日　ごじつ　**gojitsu**　at a later date

後	日										

食後　しょくご　**shokugo**　after a meal

食	後										

一年後　いちねんご　**ichinengo**　a year later

一	年	後									

五日前　いつかまえ　**itsukamae**　five days ago

五	日	前									

二日後　ふつかご　**futsukago**　two days later

二	日	後									

右カーブ　みぎカーブ　**migi kābu**　right-hand bend in the road

右	カ	ー	ブ								

左クリック　ひだりクリック　**hidari kurikku**　left click (on a mouse)

左	ク	リ	ッ	ク					

右ハンドル　みぎハンドル　**migi handoru**　right-hand drive (car)

右	ハ	ン	ド	ル					

PRACTICE 13
上 下 中 外

年上　としうえ　**toshiue**　elder

年	上										

上る　のぼる　**noboru**　to go up

上	る										

中古　ちゅうこ　**chūko**　secondhand

中	古										

年下　としした　**toshishita**　younger

年	下										

中国　ちゅうごく　**chūgoku**　China

中	国										

中山　なかやま　**Nakayama**　Nakayama (Japanese surname)

中	山										

中間　ちゅうかん　**chūkan**　the middle; intermediate

中	間										

下る　くだる　**kudaru**　to go down

下	る										

上げる　あげる　**ageru**　to raise

上	げ	る									

外れる　はずれる　**hazureru**　to come off, slip

外	れ	る									

上がる　あがる　**agaru**　to rise

上	が	る									

一日中　いちにちじゅう　**ichinichijū**　all day long

一	日	中									

下りる　おりる　**oriru**　to go down; to get off

下	り	る									

下さい　ください　**kudasai**　please give it to me

下	さ	い									

外国人　がいこくじん　**gaikokujin**　foreigner

外	国	人									

下がる　さがる　**sagaru**　to hang down, to go down

下	が	る									

中学校　ちゅうがっこう　**chūgakkō**　junior high school

中	学	校									

外出する　がいしゅつする　**gaishutsu suru**　to go out

外	出	す	る								

PRACTICE 14
北 南 東 西

東口　ひがしぐち　**higashiguchi**　east exit

東 口

北口　きたぐち　**kitaguchi**　north exit

北 口

東西　とうざい　**tōzai**　east and west

東 西

西口　にしぐち　**nishiguchi**　west exit

西 口

中東　ちゅうとう　**chūtō**　the Middle East

中 東

南口　みなみぐち　**minamiguchi**　south exit

南 口

北国　きたぐに　**kitaguni**　northern country

北 国

南西　なんせい　**nansei**　southwest

南 西

南国　なんごく　**nangoku**　southern country

南 国

北西　ほくせい　**hokusei**　northwest

北	西										

東西南北　とうざいなんぼく　**tōzainanboku**　north, south, east, west

東	西	南	北								

古今東西　ここんとうざい　**kokontōzai**　all times and places

古	今	東	西								

東南アジア　とうなんアジア　**tōnan ajia**　Southeast Asia

東	南	ア	ジ	ア					

南アメリカ　みなみアメリカ　**minami amerika**　South America

南	ア	メ	リ	カ					

北アメリカ　きたアメリカ　**kita amerika**　North America

北	ア	メ	リ	カ					

南アフリカ　みなみアフリカ　**minami afurika**　South Africa

南	ア	フ	リ	カ					

西ヨーロッパ　にしヨーロッパ　**nishi yōroppa**　Western Europe

西	ヨ	ー	ロ	ッ	パ						

東ヨーロッパ　ひがしヨーロッパ　**higashi yōroppa**　Eastern Europe

東	ヨ	ー	ロ	ッ	パ						

PRACTICE 15
白 花 川 山

川上　かわかみ　**kawakami**　upriver

川	上										

小川　おがわ　**ogawa**　stream

小	川										

川下　かわしも　**kawashimo**　downstream

川	下										

国花　こっか　**kokka**　national flower

国	花										

空白　くうはく　**kūhaku**　blank

空	白										

川口　かわぐち　**Kawaguchi**　Kawaguchi (Japanese surname)

川	口										

山道　やまみち　**yamamichi**　mountain road

山	道										

白い　しろい　**shiroi**　white

白	い										

山本　やまもと　**Yamamoto**　Yamamoto (Japanese surname)

山	本										

山口　やまぐち　**Yamaguchi**　Yamaguchi (Japanese surname)

山口

山下　やました　**Yamashita**　Yamashita (Japanese surname)

山下

白人　はくじん　**hakujin**　white person

白人

白日　はくじつ　**hakujitsu**　broad daylight

白日

花見　はなみ　**hanami**　cherry blossom viewing

花見

花たば　はなたば　**hanataba**　bouquet

花たば

生け花　いけばな　**ikebana**　ikebana (Japanese flower arranging)

生け花

山のぼり　やまのぼり　**yamanobori**　mountain climbing

山のぼり

白ワイン　しろワイン　**shirowain**　white wine

白ワイン

PRACTICE 16
空 天 気 雨

空気　くうき　**kūki**　air

空	気										

空手　からて　**karate**　karate

空	手										

空く　あく　**aku**　to become empty

空	く										

気分　きぶん　**kibun**　feeling

気	分										

人気　にんき　**ninki**　popularity

人	気										

天気　てんき　**tenki**　weather

天	気										

雨天　うてん　**uten**　rainy weather

雨	天										

小雨　こさめ　**kosame**　drizzle

小	雨										

電気　でんき　**denki**　electricity

電	気										

大雨　おおあめ　**ōame**　heavy rain

大雨

天国　てんごく　**tengoku**　paradise, heaven

天国

雨ふり　あめふり　**amefuri**　rainy weather

雨ふり

空ける　あける　**akeru**　to vacate

空ける

空っぽ　からっぽ　**karappo**　empty

空っぽ

天の川　あまのがわ　**amanogawa**　the Milky Way

天の川

気になる　きになる　**ki ni naru**　to be worried about

気になる

気がつく　きがつく　**ki ga tsuku**　to notice

気がつく

気が小さい　きがちいさい　**ki ga chīsai**　nervous, timid

気が小さい

PRACTICE 17
学 校 先 生

先生 せんせい **sensei** teacher

先	生										

先日 せんじつ **senjitsu** the other day

先	日										

学生 がくせい **gakusei** student

学	生										

学ぶ まなぶ **manabu** to study, to learn

学	ぶ										

学校 がっこう **gakkō** school

学	校										

校門 こうもん **kōmon** school gate

校	門										

大学 だいがく **daigaku** university

大	学										

高校 こうこう **kōkō** high school

高	校										

母校 ぼこう **bokō** alma mater

母	校										

校長　こうちょう　**kōchō**　school principal

校	長										

学食　がくしょく　**gakushoku**　school cafeteria

学	食										

生ゴミ　なまゴミ　**nama gomi**　kitchen garbage

生	ゴ	ミ									

生きる　いきる　**ikiru**　to live

生	き	る									

つま先　つまさき　**tsumasaki**　tip of the toe

つ	ま	先									

あて先　あてさき　**atesaki**　(destination) address

あ	て	先									

小学校　しょうがっこう　**shōgakkō**　elementary school

小	学	校									

生ビール　なまビール　**nama bīru**　draft beer

生	ビ	ー	ル								

生まれる　うまれる　**umareru**　to be born

生	ま	れ	る								

PRACTICE 18
体 本 書 読

本人　ほんにん　**hon'nin**　the person him/herself

本 人

大体　だいたい　**daitai**　more or less, just about

大 体

本日　ほじつ　**honjitsu**　today (formal)

本 日

車体　しゃたい　**shatai**　body of a car

車 体

書体　しょたい　**shotai**　font, character style

書 体

読書　どくしょ　**dokusho**　reading

読 書

人体　じんたい　**jintai**　human body

人 体

本体　ほんたい　**hontai**　body (of a machine)

本 体

中本　なかもと　**Nakamoto**　Nakamoto (Japanese surname)

中 本

気体　きたい　**kitai**　gas, vapor

気	体										

本名　ほんみょう　**honmyō**　real name

本	名										

本年　ほんねん　**hon'nen**　this year (formal)

本	年										

書く　かく　**kaku**　to write

書	く										

読む　よむ　**yomu**　to read

読	む										

書道　しょどう　**shodō**　calligraphy

書	道										

日本人　にほんじん　**Nihonjin**　Japanese person

日	本	人									

本気で　ほんきで　**honki de**　seriously

本	気	で									

読書会　どくしょかい　**dokushokai**　reading circle

読	書	会									

PRACTICE 19
見 聞 言 語

語る　かたる　**kataru**　to tell; to talk

語	る										

言語　げんご　**gengo**　language, speech

言	語										

聞く　きく　**kiku**　to listen; to ask

聞	く										

言う　いう　**iu**　to say

言	う										

語学　ごがく　**gogaku**　language study

語	学										

会見　かいけん　**kaiken**　interview

会	見										

聞き手　ききて　**kikite**　listener

聞	き	手									

見せる　みせる　**miseru**　to show, to display

見	せ	る									

見える　みえる　**mieru**　to be able to see

見	え	る									

外来語　がいらいご **gairaigo** loanword

外	来	語									

中国語　ちゅうごくご **chūgokugo** Chinese language

中	国	語									

見出し　みだし **midashi** headline, heading

見	出	し									

語り手　かたりて **katarite** narrator

語	り	手									

見学する　けんがくする **kengaku suru** to observe (for learning)

見	学	す	る								

聞こえる　きこえる **kikoeru** to hear

聞	こ	え	る								

見聞きする　みききする **mikiki suru** to see and hear

見	聞	き	す	る					

小言を言う　こごとをいう **kogoto o iu** to scold

小	言	を	言	う					

聞き上手な　ききじょうずな **kikijōzuna** good listener

聞	き	上	手	な					

PRACTICE 20
車 駅 会 社

本社　ほんしゃ　**honsha**　head office

本	社										

会社　かいしゃ　**kaisha**　company

会	社										

社会　しゃかい　**shakai**　society

社	会										

会計　かいけい　**kaikei**　bill, accounts

会	計										

駅前　えきまえ　**ekimae**　in front of the station

駅	前										

社名　しゃめい　**shamei**　company name

社	名										

新車　しんしゃ　**shinsha**　new car

新	車										

会う　あう　**au**　to meet

会	う										

社長　しゃちょう　**shachō**　president

社	長										

車道　しゃどう　**shadō**　road for cars

車	道										

電車　でんしゃ　**densha**　train

電	車										

駅長　えきちょう　**ekichō**　station master

駅	長										

中古車　ちゅうこしゃ　**chūkosha**　secondhand car

中	古	車									

社会人　しゃかいじん　**shakaijin**　member of society

社	会	人									

駅ビル　えきビル　**eki biru**　station building

駅	ビ	ル									

会計学　かいけいがく　**kaikeigaku**　accounting (study)

会	計	学									

ワゴン車　ワゴンしゃ　**wagonsha**　station wagon

ワ	ゴ	ン	車								

下車する　げしゃする　**gesha suru**　to get off (a bus, train, etc)

下	車	す	る								

PRACTICE 21
行 来 入 出

行く　いく　**iku**　to go

行 く

来る　くる　**kuru**　to come

来 る

行う　おこなう　**okonau**　to perform, to carry out

行 う

来年　らいねん　**rainen**　next year

来 年

入国　にゅうこく　**nyūkoku**　entry into a country (immigration)

入 国

出国　しゅっこく　**shukkoku**　departure from a country

出 国

入る　はいる　**hairu**　to enter

入 る

出る　でる　**deru**　to come out

出 る

出す　だす　**dasu**　to take out

出 す

行き先　いきさき　**ikisaki**　destination

行	き	先									

出来る　できる　**dekiru**　to be able

出	来	る									

入れる　いれる　**ireru**　to put in

入	れ	る									

入会する　にゅうかいする　**nyūkai suru**　to become a member of, enroll

入	会	す	る								

入学する　にゅうがくする　**nyūgaku suru**　to be admitted to a school

入	学	す	る								

来日する　らいにちする　**rainichi suru**　to come to Japan

来	日	す	る								

出入り口　でいりぐち　**deiriguchi**　entrance and exit

出	入	り	口								

出かける　でかける　**dekakeru**　to go out

出	か	け	る								

出来上がる　できあがる　**dekiagaru**　to be completed

出	来	上	が	る					

PRACTICE 22
国 道 安 高

安い　やすい　**yasui**　cheap

安	い										

高さ　たかさ　**takasa**　height

高	さ										

高い　たかい　**takai**　high; expensive

高	い										

外国　がいこく　**gaikoku**　foreign country

外	国										

国外　こくがい　**kokugai**　overseas, abroad

国	外										

国名　こくめい　**kokumei**　country name

国	名										

高木　たかぎ　**Tagaki**　Takagi (Japanese surname)

高	木										

国道　こくどう　**kokudō**　national highway

国	道										

国土　こくど　**kokudo**　country, territory

国	土										

小道　こみち　**komichi**　lane, path

小	道										

道学　どうがく　**dōgaku**　Confucianism

道	学										

ドル高　ドルだか　**dorudaka**　a rise in value of the dollar

ド	ル	高									

ドル安　ドルやす　**doruyasu**　a drop in value of the dollar

ド	ル	安									

名高い　なだかい　**nadakai**　renowned

名	高	い									

国立大学　こくりつだいがく　**kokuritsu daigaku**　a national university

国	立	大	学								

安っぽい　やすっぽい　**yasuppoi**　cheap looking

安	っ	ぽ	い								

安くする　やすくする　**yasuku suru**　to knock the price down

安	く	す	る								

安らかな　やすらかな　**yasurakana**　untroubled, at ease

安	ら	か	な								

PRACTICE 23
飲 食 魚 長

金魚　きんぎょ　**kingyo**　goldfish

金　魚

人魚　にんぎょ　**ningyo**　mermaid

人　魚

小魚　こざかな　**kozakana**　small fish

小　魚

会長　かいちょう　**kaichō**　chairperson

会　長

長い　ながい　**nagai**　long

長　い

長さ　ながさ　**nagasa**　length

長　さ

飲む　のむ　**nomu**　to drink

飲　む

長女　ちょうじょ　**chōjo**　eldest daughter

長　女

食道　しょくどう　**shokudō**　esophagus

食　道

食前　しょくぜん　**shokuzen**　before meals

食前

外食　がいしょく　**gaishoku**　eating out

外食

飲食　いんしょく　**inshoku**　eating and drinking

飲食

学長　がくちょう　**gakuchō**　university president

学長

飲み水　のみみず　**nomimizu**　drinking water

飲み水

食べる　たべる　**taberu**　to eat

食べる

食べもの　たべもの　**tabemono**　food

食べもの

飲みもの　のみもの　**nomimono**　beverage

飲みもの

飲みに行く　のみにいく　**nomi ni iku**　to go drinking

飲に行く

PRACTICE 24
古 新 小 大

新人 しんじん **shinjin** newcomer

新	人										

古本 ふるほん **furuhon** secondhand (used) book

古	本										

お古 おふる **ofuru** hand-me-downs

お	古										

新聞 しんぶん **shinbun** newspaper

新	聞										

大小 だいしょう **daishō** large and small

大	小										

古い ふるい **furui** old

古	い										

大川 おおかわ **Ōkawa** Okawa (Japanese surname)

大	川										

小山 こやま **Koyama** Koyama (Japanese surname)

小	山										

大西 おおにし **Ōnishi** Onishi (Japanese surname)

大	西										

大会　たいかい　**taikai**　convention, mass meeting

大	会										

新年　しんねん　**shin'nen**　the New Year

新	年										

新しい　あたらしい　**atarashii**　new

新	し	い									

新入生　しんにゅうせい　**shin'nyūsei**　new student

新	入	生									

小エビ　こエビ　**ko ebi**　shrimp (small)

小	エ	ビ									

大きい　おおきい　**ōkii**　big

大	き	い									

小さい　ちいさい　**chīsai**　small

小	さ	い									

小学生　しょうがくせい　**shōgakusei**　elementary school student

小	学	生									

小づかい　こづかい　**kozukai**　pocket money

小	づ	か	い								

PRACTICE 25
少 多 買 電

多少　たしょう　**tashō**　kind of, somewhat

多	少										

多い　おおい　**o'oi**　many

多	い										

多分　たぶん　**tabun**　perhaps

多	分										

少し　すこし　**sukoshi**　a little

少	し										

買う　かう　**kau**　to buy

買	う										

電子　でんし　**denshi**　electron

電	子										

少食　しょうしょく　**shōshoku**　light eating

少	食										

買い手　かいて　**kaite**　buyer

買	い	手									

多大な　ただいな　**tadai na**　considerable, significant (amount)

多	大	な									

電子学　でんしがく **denshigaku** electronics (study)

電	子	学									

少ない　すくない **sukunai** few

少	な	い									

年少の　ねんしょうの **nenshō no** young, juvenile

年	少	の									

買いもの　かいもの **kaimono** shopping

買	い	も	の								

電気会社　でんきがいしゃ **denki gaisha** electric company

電	気	会	社								

少年少女　しょうねんしょうじょ **shōnen shōjo** boys and girls

少	年	少	女								

電子レンジ　でんしレンジ **denshi renji** microwave oven

電	子	レ	ン	ジ					

電子タバコ　でんしタバコ **denshi tabako** electronic cigarette

電	子	タ	バ	コ					

電気ショック　でんきショック **denki shokku** electric shock

電	気	シ	ョ	ッ	ク						

PRACTICE 26
名 立

名人　めいじん　**meijin**　master, expert

名	人										

名前　なまえ　**namae**　name

名	前										

立つ　たつ　**tatsu**　to stand

立	つ										

名言　めいげん　**meigen**　famous words

名	言										

立体の　りったいの　**rittai no**　three-dimensional

立	体	の									

国立の　こくりつの　**kokuritsu no**　national

国	立	の									

ファイル名　ファイルめい　**fairu mei**　(computer) filename

フ	ァ	イ	ル	名					

立ち会い人　たちあいにん　**tachiainin**　witness

立	ち	会	い	人					

立ち上げる　たちあげる　**tachiageru**　to boot up (a computer)

立	ち	上	げ	る					

Radical Index

Readings Index

Japanese–English Index

English–Japanese Index